Henry M. Dexter

The True Story of John Smyth - the Se-Baptist

As told by himself and his contemporaries - with an inquiry whether dipping were a new mode of baptism in England, in or about 1641

Henry M. Dexter

The True Story of John Smyth - the Se-Baptist
As told by himself and his contemporaries - with an inquiry whether dipping were a new mode of baptism in England, in or about 1641

ISBN/EAN: 9783337182410

Printed in Europe, USA, Canada, Australia, Japan

Cover: Foto ©Lupo / pixelio.de

More available books at **www.hansebooks.com**

The True Story of John Smyth,

THE SE-BAPTIST,

AS TOLD BY HIMSELF AND HIS CONTEMPORARIES;

WITH AN INQUIRY

Whether Dipping were a New Mode of Baptism in England, in or about 1641;

AND

SOME CONSIDERATION OF THE HISTORICAL VALUE OF
CERTAIN EXTRACTS FROM THE ALLEGED

"Ancient Records"

OF THE BAPTIST CHURCH OF EPWORTH, CROWLE, AND BUTTERWICK (ENG.), LATELY PUBLISHED, AND
CLAIMED TO SUGGEST IMPORTANT MODIFICATIONS OF THE HISTORY OF THE 17TH CENTURY.

With Collections toward a Bibliography of the first two generations of the Baptist Controversy.

By HENRY MARTYN DEXTER.

BOSTON:
LEE AND SHEPARD,
1881.

Copyright, 1881, by H. M. DEXTER.

Stereotyped by Thomas Todd, Congregational House, Boston.

TO

BROWN UNIVERSITY AND YALE COLLEGE:

By Diploma

FROM EACH OF WHICH

THE AUTHOR HAS THE HONOR TO BE A "MASTER OF ARTS,"

AND

BY THE TRAINING OF EACH OF WHICH THROUGH ONE HALF OF THE COLLEGE COURSE

HE HOPES NOT TO HAVE BEEN WHOLLY UNFITTED TO BE, IF NOT A MASTER, YET A

SCRUPULOUS PRACTICER, OF THE ART OF CLEARLY SEEING AND FAIRLY

STATING THE TRUTH OF MATTERS, AS TO WHICH

BAPTISTS AND CONGREGATIONALISTS, IN CONSCIENCE, FEELING AND ACTION,

HAVE DIFFERED;

This Discussion is Affectionately Dedicated.

44. In fourtie Dayes, they wrote two hundred and four Bookes.

45. And when the fourtie Dayes were fulfilled, the Most High spake, saying: The first that thou hast written, publish openly, that the worthie and vnworthie may reade it.

46. But keep ye seuentie last, that thou maiest giue them to the wise among thy People.

47. For in them is the Veine of Vnderstanding, and the Fountaine of Wisdome, and the Riuer of Knowledge.

48. And I did soe.

If thou canst bring Algummim trees to the Worke of the Temple, I pray thee do it: my Firre shall giue place — and how canst thou require more of mee?

INTRODUCTION.

IT need hardly be said that the subjects herein discussed I do not now approach for the first time. The very circumstance that some former judgments in regard to them have been questioned by most respectable critics, together with the desire to exhume from the literature of the past the means of fairly concluding, if possible, the discussion, led me to take advantage of a few days of leisure during the past winter in London to restudy them. I herewith submit the results with some confidence on two points, viz.: first, that I am able to introduce into the case not merely valuable but decisive new testimony; and, second, that there is small probability of further important addition to the roll of witnesses. I have — so far as I am aware, for the first time — attempted some Bibliographical account of the Baptist controversy in England from 1640 to 1700 inclusive; and, while I am far from supposing the result to be complete, I am disposed to think that it includes every utterance of much consequence on every side. And, having personally made close examination of something like *seventy-five per cent.* of the volumes therein catalogued; including nearly or quite every treatise likely to be of special value toward settling points in controversy; I cannot anticipate much new light as likely to dawn from sources still remaining occult.

I believe it to be a principle more and more establishing itself in the conviction of students of history, that concerning any remote period contemporary evidence where it can be had, fairly weighed, must always take precedence of the statements of set histories written long afterward, and, from necessity, and perhaps the fashion of the times, made up more largely from tradition and the reminiscences of the aged, than from the sifting of original records, or the exhaustive examination of the controversial writings of the period under review. To take the case in hand: it was not until 1738 — from three to four generations after the occurrences first to be narrated — that Thomas Crosby began to publish that *History of the English Baptists* which has been naturally taken as chief authority on the matters which it treats; while in various ways he makes it clear, not only that he never consulted, but that he never even came to the knowledge of the existence of, a large majority of the more than four hundred volumes, which, between 1640 and the close of that century, had been published upon the mode and subjects of baptism, with the personal and other issues thereto related. His discussion of the question whether John Smyth baptized himself [i: 91-100] is avowedly founded upon a few extracts from Smyth's treatises and those of his opponents as found at second-hand in a book published after he had been in his grave seventy-eight years; strengthened by the writer's conjecture that John Robinson and others were so imbittered against the poor man that they could hardly be expected to tell the truth concerning him. It can surely admit of

(v)

small question that such "history" as that, can now have value only as its conclusions may be confirmed by books and manuscripts still remaining from the pen of the Se-baptist himself, and those who discussed his notions with him. The same principle holds as to the question whether Dipping were introduced in or about 1641, as a new mode of baptism, by English churches which had previously been differenced from their Separatist brethren only by rejecting the baptism of infants, without controversy as to the manner in which the rite should be administered. If such were the fact, we cannot fail to find traces of it in the tracts — of which, as will be seen, I have traced more than one hundred in the first five years — which swarmed from licensed and secret presses, on that general subject. In their pages, and not in the vague and possibly not wholly unprejudiced surmises of Crosby ninety-six years after, and of Ivimey one hundred and sixty-nine years after, and of others still later, the truth is most likely to be found; as a single pertinent illustration of which may be named the fact that Ivimey [i: 157] and Brook [iii: 399] represent Praise-God Barbon as a Baptist minister, while his own books [Nos. 6 and 18, *Appendix*] show him as writing against the Baptists.

Speaking of prejudice, I am reminded that my own labor herein has been much increased by the fact that on former occasions I have been so unfortunate as to receive censure from Baptist critics; some of whom have not hesitated to intimate that my sectarian bias is so strong as to render me incapable of ordinary fairness in the treatment of such subjects. This "excellent oil" has not broken my head. I am humbly sorry if there have been any desert on my part of such censure in the past; while I am sure that the remembrance of these adverse criticisms has in my renewed investigations stimulated me to an indefatigable anxiety as to three points, viz.: to get at all the truth; to estimate that truth with absolute impartiality; and to record the results of that estimate in the exactest manner. As to every matter touched by this investigation I can heartily adopt the language of Dr. Evans [*Early English Baptists*, etc. i: 204]: "to us it is of no moment whether it be true or false, beyond the interest which we have in it as an historical fact." Whether John Smyth baptized himself; whether Dipping were, or were not, in the last ten years of the first half of the seventeenth century, a mode of Baptism new to England; and whether the Crowle papers are veritable ancient records or a witless modern fraud; are questions which at no point touch anything vital to — I might even say, anything reasonably cherished with especial tenderness by — either Baptist or Pædobaptist believers. There would seem therefore to be no good reason why they should not be studied in as dry a light, and issued with as frigid a candor, as if they had their being in the domain of metaphysics, and not of history. In such temper I have — not without diligence and prayer — sought, in the fear of God and the love of truth, to write; having, in every case, directed all who may be disposed to doubt or criticise my conclusions to the exact sources from which they have been derived. Can it be presumptuous, or offensive, if I respectfully ask my Baptist brethren to meet me with a like spirit, in the examination of what I have written? H. M. D.

Greystones, New Bedford, Mass., 1 November, 1881.

CONTENTS.

	PAGE
CHAPTER I. THE TRUE STORY OF JOHN SMYTH, THE SE-BAPTIST; AS TOLD BY HIMSELF AND HIS CONTEMPORARIES	1-38
His birth and training	1
Beneficed at Gainsborough-on-Trent	1
Resigns his living and gathers a separate church at Gainsborough . .	2
Emigrates to Amsterdam	2
What sort of a man he was	3
His first church difficulty, and its cause	5
His own statement of the case	7
When did his change of conviction as to baptism take place? . . .	8
Testimony of Clyfton, Ainsworth, Bradford, Bernard, etc. and of Smyth himself	9–10
What modes of baptism were then prevalent, and which mode did Smyth and his company probably make use of?	10–26
Baptism by affusion clearly existed by 100 years after the Apostles .	11
Testimony of Cyprian	11
Clement V. and the 2d Council of Ravenna	12
Lyndewood, and the two prayer-books of Edward VI.	12
Calvin's view, and that of Thomas Becon	13
While the rubric enjoined immersion in England, it was the practice there in the time of our fathers to affuse, or asperge	14
View of Zuingli, and of the Helvetic, Belgic and Bohemian Confessions	15
The French Reformed and Lutheran Churches	16
Description by Sir William Brereton of a Dutch baptism	17
The original Anabaptists did not immerse	17
Hoornbeek, Hortensius, Guy de Bres, and *Een Nieu Liedeken* . . .	18
Robert Baylie's statement	19
Illustration of ancient Anabaptist baptism from an old print	20
The *Collegianten* (in 1619) the first to immerse in Holland	21
The Mennonites, though Baptists, did not dip	21
Fonts of 16th and 17th centuries not adapted to adult immersion . .	23
Washing the word ordinarily applied to the rite	24
Did Mr. Smyth first affuse himself, and then administer the ordinance to his associates?	26
His view was that the true [*i.e.* believer's] baptism had died out of the world	27
He thought a church covenanting together could re-originate it . . .	27

CHAPTER I. (*Continued.*)

	PAGE
Why he did not seek affusion from the Mennonites	28
He, and his, first disbanded their former church, and gave up their offices	29
Probable *modus operandi* of the se-baptism	30
Evidences of eight witnesses cognizant of the facts, that Smyth first baptized himself and then his company	31–33
Further testimony	33–35
The brief remainder of his story	35–38
Smyth excluded from his own Baptist church, and the reasons	36
Refused admission by the Mennonites	37
Death of Smyth (in 1612) of consumption, and burial	38

CHAPTER II. AN INQUIRY WHETHER DIPPING WERE A NEW MODE OF BAPTISM IN ENGLAND IN, OR ABOUT, 1641 ... 39–62

Baptist impressions to the contrary	39
The King's Pamphlets as a source of evidence	40
Earliest date of public Confession of immersion	41
At least eleven General Baptist Churches which did not dip	42
The case of Mr. Spilsbury's church in Wapping in 1633	43
Mr. Spilsbury did not go to Holland for Baptism	44
First reference to any novel administration of the rite	46
Twenty witnesses that dipping was a "new way," etc.	46–53
Proof that it was introduced about 1641	49
Was dipping in England originated from Holland?	53–56
Were the candidates at first in England dipped naked?	56–59
Circumstantial account of a dipping at Hemel Hempstead (1646)	60
Specimen of the debate in 1644	61

CHAPTER III. SOME CONSIDERATION OF THE HISTORICAL VALUE OF THE ALLEGED "ANCIENT RECORDS" OF THE BAPTIST CHURCH OF CROWLE, ETC. ... 63–86

Statement as to those papers, and how they became public	63
A transcript thereof	64–67
Rev. Mr. Stutterd's certificate of the genuineness of that transcript	68
Criticism of the Covenant	69
Miscellaneous blunders in little things	70–72
Blunders as to Samuel Fuller	72
Blunders as to Edward Winslow	73
Blunders as to John Carver	74
Blunders as to John Norcott	74
Blunders as to John Murton	75
Blunders as to William Bradford	76
Blunders as to William Brewster	77
Blunders as to John Smyth	78
Correspondence as to these "records"	82–83
These "records" a base forgery, at some date since 1856	84
The immense and unrelieved stupidity thereof	86

BIBLIOGRAPHICAL APPENDIX ... 87

CHAPTER I.

THE TRUE STORY OF JOHN SMYTH, THE SE-BAPTIST; AS TOLD BY HIMSELF AND HIS CONTEMPORARIES.

THE John Smyth with whom we are now concerned must have been born early in the second half of the sixteenth century, and probably of parents who were not in affluent circumstances, inasmuch as he first emerges to view when matriculating at Christ's College, Cambridge, as a sizar[1] 26 Nov. 1571. He proceeded B.A. in 1575-6, and was chosen Fellow, and commenced M.A. in 1579.[2] Francis Johnson was here, at one time, his tutor.[3] He appears to have been the Master of Arts of this name who, as we learn from Strype,[4] on the first day of Lent, 1585, preached at Cambridge a doctrine of Sabbath-keeping so much in advance of the public sentiment of the time, as to lead to his citation before the Vice Chancellor in the great chamber. He was clearly, however, not, as has been alleged,[5] the Rev. Mr. Smith who, in 1592, was confined eleven months in the Marshalsea; because the name of that sufferer was William.[6] He is next heard from, vaguely, on the authority of John Cotton, as preacher to the city of Lincoln.[7] He appears to have been afterward beneficed at Gainsborough-on-Trent.[8] We have his own statement that before separating from the Establishment he passed through nine months of doubt, and study;[9] and once held, in Coventry, with Masters Dod, Hildersham and Barbon, a conference "about withdrawing

---

[1] A *sizar* at Cambridge—like a *batteler* at Oxford—was a student who waited on the Fellows, etc. and ate after them at the public table without charge; who was therefore often, and perhaps usually, the child of parents too poor to bear his college expenses.

[2] These dates have been verified from the original MS. Records of the University, now to be consulted in the Registry Office in the Pitt Press Building, Cambridge, Eng.

[3] Gov. Bradford, *Dialogue*, etc. in Young, *Plym. Chron.* 450; Bernard, *Plaine Euidences*, etc. 19; Cotton, *Way of Cong. Chhs. Cleared*, etc. 7.

[4] *Annals of the Reformation*, etc. iii (1): 496.

[5] Hunter says this, *Founders of New Plymouth*, etc. 35; and Barclay [*Inner Life of the Religious Societies of the Commonwealth*, etc. 52]; while Waddington [*Congregational History*, etc. ii: 157] falls into the same confusion between individuals.

[6] F. Johnson, *Letter to Lord Burghley*, Lansdowne *MSS.* lxxv: 50; F. Johnson, *Answer to M. H. Jacob His Defence*, etc. 200.

[7] "As for Master Smith he standeth and falleth to his own Master; whilst he was preacher to the citie of Lincolne, he wrought with God there." *Reply to Mr. Williams, his Examination*, etc. 58.

[8] Brook [*Lives of the Puritans*, etc. ii: 196]. This takes confirmation from the fact that Bernard [*Plaine Euidences*, etc. 21] says Smyth "was made minister by Bishop Wickam;" and Wm. Wickham was Bishop of Lincoln, the diocese in which Gainsborough is, from 1584 to 1595.

[9] *Paralleles, Censvres, Observations*, etc. 128.

(1)

from true Churches, Ministers and VVorship, corrupted."[10] Possibly as early as 1602, or thereabouts,[11] he gathered a separate church at Gainsborough, of which he subsequently became pastor.[12] And, probably in 1606, with his little flock he emigrated to Amsterdam, in Holland, in search of some liberty of conscience and worship denied them at home.[13] A Barrowist church, composed of English Separatists most of whom had removed thither from London, had been there before them, certainly since 1595;[14] of which Francis Johnson was pastor and Henry Ainsworth teacher; and which, having outlived sore trials in its earlier years, had now grown to a considerable size, and, in its humble way, reached a fair degree of outward prosperity. Here Smyth and his people established themselves, by the side of the older residents, as the "Second English Church at Amsterdam."[15]

---

[10] *Way of Cong. Chhs. Cleared*, etc. 7; *Paralleles*, etc. 129.

[11] The sole authority for this date is Morton [*N. E. Memoriall*, etc. 1], as confirmed by him in the margin of Bradford's Sketch of Brewster, copied from the Governor's MSS. upon the Plymouth Church Records. [Young, *Plym. Chron.* etc. 465.] Prince [*Annals*, etc. Pt. i: 4] accepts the date on the theory that although unmentioned by Bradford, Morton had recovered it "from some other Writings . . . or from Oral Conference." Though rather early, this is not an impossible year, and Hunter [*Founders*, etc. 89] seems to favor it.

[12] Here again Bernard (his neighbor) testifies [*Plaine Evidences*, etc. 21]: "By and by in Brownisme he renounced [his Church of England ministry] & was made Minister by Tradesmen, and called himselfe *The Pastour of the Church at Gainsborough.*"

[13] Evans [i: 202], Ivimey [*Hist. Eng. Bap.* etc. i: 114] and Taylor [*Hist. Gen. Bap.* etc. i: 67] concur in naming 1606 as the year of this exodus. On the other hand Smyth writes himself "Pastor off the church at Ganesburgh" in a letter which [*Paralleles*, etc. 2] it would seem must have been written at some time in 1607, and might thence naturally imply that he and the church were there then. The first fixed point which seems to be determinable at Amsterdam from which to measure back is found in this remark by Smyth [*Character of the Beast*, etc. 71]: "I end writing this 24 of March, 1608." But his *Paralleles*, etc., and his *Diferences* (both published before he led his church into a new baptism) had been issued before this, with time enough afterward to allow the full development of that new theory and practice of adult baptism which it is the object of the *Character of the Beast*, etc. to explain and defend. I scarcely see how all this could have taken place, with the necessary intervals of time, unless the company had reached Amsterdam before 1607. Prof. Scheffer, who has studied the whole subject on the ground with masterly skill, puts the arrival in the autumn of 1606. [*De Brownisten Te Amsterdam*, etc. (1881) p. 85.] "Na aldus voor de achterblijvenden te hebben gezorgd, besloot Smyth tot den overtocht en kwam te Amsterdam in 't late najaar, denkelijk October of November 1606."

[14] See *Congregationalism of last Three Hundred Years, as Seen in its Literature*, etc. 255-311.

[15] I was in error in a former volume [*Congregationalism, as Seen*, etc. 312] in the statement adopted too hastily from *Brook* [ii: 196] and *Barclay* [63, 68] that Smyth and his people first joined themselves to the church of Johnson and Ainsworth. Subsequent investigation and reflection have convinced me that Smyth himself, and Gov. Bradford, are more trustworthy witnesses. The language of the latter seems almost necessarily to imply the coexistence from the beginning of the two churches, thus:

"He [Smyth] was some time pastor to a company of honest and godly men which came with him out of England, and pitched at Amsterdam." *Dialogue*, etc. in *Young*, etc. 450.

"Seeing how Mr. John Smith and his companie was allready fallen in to contention with ye church yt was ther before them . . . and also that ye flames of contention were like to breake out in yt anciente church it selfe, etc." *Hist. Plim. Plant.* 16.

Smyth himself, in the title-page of his *Diferences of the Churches of the Seperation*, etc. published during the year of Bradford's residence in Amsterdam, calls the body to whom he ministered, "the Brethren of the Seperation of the Second English Church at Amsterdam;" while I think Ainsworth's language [*Animadversion*, etc. 137] may be naturally explained without the theory that when Smyth "proffered vvritings," and Johnson "vvithstood and refused that course," they were members of the same church.

It may be well to pause here to get, if we may, some suggestive glimpse of the kind of person whose life we are investigating. Clearly he was an impulsive man, with something magnetic in his popular sympathies and gifts strongly attaching his friends to himself;[16] able to turn his hand to more than one thing;[17] unselfish[18] and charitable;[19] punctilious and courageous; never ashamed to own any wrong in himself which he discovered;[20] a good preacher, and a scholar of considerable acquirements[21] — having, in short, many of the elements of a great and good man. On the other hand his mind was restless, and perhaps his conscience morbidly sensitive to small matters, so that his extreme defect came to be a want of stability — not of purpose, but in the relation of his perceptions and volitions to the data on which, as a foundation, purposes stand. Gov. Bradford, no doubt as truly as tersely described him as to this, when he said: "his inconstancy, and unstable judgment, and being so suddenly carried away with things, did soon overthrow him."[22] Robinson went so far as severely to blame him for yielding to this temperament: "for Mr. Smyth, his instability & wantonnes of wit is his syn, & our crosse."[23]

It would appear to have been one of Mr. Smyth's latest labors in the north of England, or one of his earliest works in Amsterdam,[24] to put to press a small tract of two and thirty pages entitled *Principles and Inferences concerning the visible Church;* which in style is dense and clear, which bristles with proof-texts after the fashion of the time, and which in sentiment shows him at the period of its authorship to have been essentially in thorough accord with the

---

[16] Even the company which felt itself compelled to the extreme course of excommunicating him for theological error, said of him, afterward:

"Let no man think that we could not willingly have undergone that reproach, and far greater, to have still enjoyed him: yea, what would we not have endured or done; would we not have lost all we had, yea, would we not have plucked out our eyes; would we not have laid down our lives? Doth not God know this? Do not men know it? Doth not he know it? Have we not neglected ourselves, our wives, our children and all we had, and respected him? And we confess we had good cause so to do in respect of those most excellent gifts and graces of God that then did abound in him; and all our love was too little for him, and not worthy of him." *Declaration of Faith of English People,* etc. (Helwys's Company) (1611) 14.

[17] "After a certaine time (living at Amsterdam) he began to practise Physicke (knowing that a man was bound to vse the gifts that the lord had bestowed vppon him for the Good of others), in administering whereof, he vsually tooke nothing of the poorer sort: and if they were rich, he tooke but haife so much as other Doctors did, etc." *Declaration of Faith of English People,* etc. (Smyth's Company) (1612) 44.

[18] "I neuer received of them [his church] all put together the value of fortie shillings to my knowledge, since I came out of England." *Ibid.* 40.

[19] "Moreover he was so mindefull, and so carefull for the poore: that he would rather live sparingly in his house (or as we say) neglect himself, his wife, and children then that anie should be in extremitie. Vppon a time seeing one slenderly apparelled, he sent them his gowne to make them clothes, etc." *Ibid.* 43.

[20] "In this writing something ther is which overwharteth my former judgment in some treaties by me formerly published: Yet I would intreat the reader not to impute that as a fault unto mee; rather it should be accounted a vertue to retract errors. Know therfor that latter thoughts oft tymes are better then the former, & I do professe this (that no man account it straunge) that I will every day as my errors shall be discovered confesse them & renounce them." [*Differences of the Churches of the Separation,* etc. iv.] "I have often tymes beene accused of inconstancie: well, let them think of mee as they please, I professe I have changed, and shallbe readie still to change for the better." *Last Booke of John Smith,* etc. 31.

[21] "A good preacher, and of other good parts." Bradford, *Dialogue,* etc. 450.

[22] *Ibid.* 450.

[23] *Justification of Separation,* etc. 58.

[24] It is dated 1607, and in type and ornament it appears to resemble some other issues of the Amsterdam press of that period.

Amsterdam Separatists; with possibly a slight leaning toward the Brownist, in distinction from the Barrowist, theory of the distribution of Church power.[25] This was almost immediately followed by a larger work — designed to reply to some passages of Bernard in his *Separatists Schisme*, and still further to vindicate the Congregational way. When Mr. Smyth wrote this[26] he was no Baptist; for again and again in its pages he refers to them in terms of reprobation.[27] Nor had he yet obtained those new views on other points which were soon to cause the severance of fellowship with the "ancient" church, and which it was to be the object of his next treatise to set forth and establish. Down to this date he heartily accepted the ordinary doctrines of the Separatists; maintaining them "to be the vndoubted truth of God;" not indeed repudiating for them the name "Brownisme,"[28] and going even further than in his previous work in advocacy of the practical democracy of Brownism over the semi-Presbyterianism of the Barrowism which then prevailed.[29]

It must have been, I think, early in 1608, that this persistent rover

"to fresh woods, and pastures new"

began vigorously to persuade his church that hitherto they had all been wrong on one vital point, as to which reform needed to be immediate. It has been usual to represent that the movement which now took place was a secession from the "ancient" church, and was caused by the adoption of new views as

---

[25] "Election is by most voyces of the members of the Church in ful communion. . . . Ordination and so imposition of hands apperteyneth to the whole church, as doth election and approbation, yet for order sake the fittest members lay on hands and perform al other the particulars of ordination for & in the name of the whole church." *Principles and Inferences*, etc. 15, 17.

[26] *Paralleles, Censures, Observations*, etc. n. pl. 4°. pp. iii, 136, xii. The title-page says "Printed 1609." Its type does not resemble that of other Amsterdam issues of that date which I have seen, while "The Printer to the Reader" on the last page may naturally imply that it was not issued under its author's eye. I conjecture therefore — not without some corroboration from its pages — that it had been written a year or two previous, circulated in MS. and then came into type without Mr. Smyth's immediate volition, and probably at a time when it no longer fairly reflected his views.

[27] E. g. "Do you think that God accepteth the prayers & Religious exercises of the Papists, the Arrians, the *Anabaptists*, the Familists, or *any other heretiques or Antichristians!*" [p. 13.] "Neither can *a wicked company* be called Holy or Saints truly in respect of the visible signes of Gods favour or presence, For then the Papists, *Anabaptists*, Familists, Arrians, & other *Heretiques* should truly be calcd Saints, seing they have the word & Sacraments among them," etc. etc. [p. 35.]

[28] *Paralleles*, etc. [135.] So [109] "You say wee are not to bee heard, bicause (as Brownists) wee speake our owne fantasies, & visions of our owne harts, and are obstinate. Wel Mr. Bern. [ard] I say no more for this point, but this, that every Godly mynded man give sentence whither you or wee have the truth."

[29] "You are to remēber that Christs church in several respects is a Monarchie, an Aristocraty, a Democratie. In respect of Christ the King it is a Monarchy, of the Eldership an Aristocratie, of the brethren joyntly a Democratie or Popular government. . . wee say therefore that the body of the Church hath all powre immediately from Christ: and the Elders have al their powre from the body of the Church, which powre of the Eldership is not exerciced, nor can not be vsed over or against the whole body of the Church, for that is an Antichristian vsurpation. . . VVee say that the definitive sentence, the determining powre, the negative voice is in the body of the Church, not in the Elders," etc. 54, 55.

to baptism by Mr. Smyth and his sympathizers. In a former volume [30] I was misled as to the first point, while, as to the second, taking pains to show not only that the moving cause had no reference to the question of baptism, but that Smyth himself was not as yet a Baptist. Further evidence has made it clear that there was at this time no separation from the first church on the part of Smyth and his friends, and no forming of a second church by them; for the best of all reasons that the Gainsborough company had never become merged in the "ancient" church, but had been a second church by themselves — in close communion with the first — from their arrival in Amsterdam. What really took place now therefore was that Smyth led his second church to decline all further communion with the "ancient" church under Johnson and Ainsworth, until it should renounce and forsake that "mysterie of iniquitie" which yet remained in its "worship and offices," wherein "Antichrist is not utterlie eyther revealed or abolished, but in a verie high degree exalted."[31] As it is a matter of some consequence to determine exactly what the issue between them at this date was, and as the evidence which I adduced when treating the subject two years ago has been held insufficient,[32] I now ask my readers' attention to two or three further witnesses on the point. And in the first place I will cite Mr. Ainsworth, who, writing less than a twelvemonth after, on the spot, thus spake concerning it:[33]

Ther was one onely difference betweene M. Smyth and us, when firſt he began to quarrel; though ſynce he haue increaſt them, and increaſeth dayly, with deadly feud and open oppoſition, as al men may ſee.

That difference was this. He with his followers breaking off cōmunion with us, charged us with ſynn for uſing our Engliſh Bibles in the worſhip of God; & he thought that the teachers should bring the originals, the Hebrew and Greek, and out of them tranſlate by voice. His principal reaſon againſt our tranſlated ſcripture was this. No Apocrypha writing but only the Canonical ſcriptures, are to be uſed in the church in time of Gods worſhip. Every written tranſlation is an Apocrypha writing, & is not canonicall ſcripture. Therefore every written tranſlation is unlawful in the church in time of Gods worſhip. Why he counteth every tranſlation Apocrypha, and what he meant therby, appeareth by theſe words of his: a written tranſlation (ſayth he), or interpretation, is as wel & as much an humane writing, as an homilie or prayer, written & read. . . That this point of the tranſlation was [at first] the *onely* difference, as it is known to al that then heard his publik proteſ-

---

[30] *Congregationalism of last Three Hundred Years*, etc. 312.
[31] *Diferences of Chh's. of Separation*, etc. i.
[32] I refer particularly to an editorial judgment in the Chicago *Standard* of 1 July, 1880, which stigmatizes "the points named" as "trivial." The *Examiner and Chronicle* of 19 Aug. 1880, also said of my conclusion that it "seems to be based on partial and incomplete evidence."
[33] *A Defence of the Holy Scriptures, Worſhip and Miniſterie uſed in the Chriſtian churches ſeparated from Antichriſt: againſt the challenges, cavils, and contradiction of Mr. Smyth*. Amsterdam, 1609. [4°. pp. iv, 132.] [B. M. (4103. d.)] pp. 1–3.

tatiō; fo his words in writing fhew it. . . . So if wee would have layd afide our tranflated Bibles, communion (they fay) fhould have been kept with us. . . .

After much time fpent about this controverfie, he manifefted other differences, touching the minifterie and treafurie, etc.

Mr. Bernard also, then at Worksop — scarcely more than twenty miles, as the crow flies, from Smyth's old Gainsborough parish — and who had known him well, after sketching previous steps in his career, thus refers to this period, in a volume written within two years:[34]

Sixthly, . . hee holdeth for truths what Mr. *Ainfworth* in his Anfwer to me rejecteth for errors: Hee iudgeth their worfhip in part Iudaifme, their Minifterie and Gouernment Anti-Chriftian; of which hee hath alfo publifhed a Booke, etc.

About the same time Richard Clyfton, who had been the Teacher of the church of which John Robinson was pastor and William Brewster elder, published a little quarto at Amsterdam, where he was a co-resident with Smyth during the events now passing under review, in which he states the cause of the change which took place in the second church to be:[35]

Firft, calling into queftion, whether the fcriptures being tranflated into other tongues, were not the writings of men. Then cafting the reading of them out of the worfhip of God, affirming that there is no better warrant to bring tranflations of Scripture into the Church, and to read them as parts and helps of worfhip, then to bring in expofitions, paraphrafts and fermons vpon the Scripture, feing all thefe are equally humane in refpect of the worke, equally divine in refpect of the matter they handle. And for the fame caufe feparated themfelves from other Churches [*i.e.* the "ancient" church of Johnson and Ainsworth, and the Scrooby-Leyden church under Robinson] that did read and vfe the fame in their publike meetings.

We may now in the light of these corroborative testimonies [36] profitably examine the statement of reasons which Smyth himself gave, at the time, in the volume which he then published in justification of the action taken by

---

[34] *Plaine Euidences: The Church of England is Apoftolicall; the Separation fchismaticall, directed againft Mr. Ainfworth the Separatist, and Mr. Smyth the fe-baptist,* etc. 1610. [4°. pp. xvi, 340.] [B. M (4135 a)] p. 19.

[35] *The Plea for Infants and Elder People, concerning their Baptifme. Or a Proceffe of the Paffages between Mr. Iohn Smyth and Richard Clyfton,* etc. Anifterdam, 1610. [4°. pp. xx, 228.] [B. M. (4323. b.)] p. v.

[36] Add to them the following from Robert Baylie's *Diffuafive From the Errours of the Time,* etc. [p. 16]:

There he [Smyth] perfevered not long in concord with his Elder Brethren of the Separation, but quickly accufed them all of Idolatry in their worfhip, for looking upon their Bibles in the time of Preaching, and on their Pfalters in the time of finging; and of Antichriftianifm in their Government, becaufe in their Prefbytery they joyned to Paftors other two Officers, Doctours and ruling Elders, which to him were humane inventions.

And this from a careful writer on the ground, within a generation [John Hoornbeck, *Summa Controverfiarum Religionis,* etc. (1653) 740]:

Sed cum antiquioribus ejufdem fectae [ille, *Smyth,*] non diu concors, quos idololatriae accufabat, quod tum in concione ad volumen Bibliorum, tum inter cantandum, Pfalterium refpicerent. etiam Antichriftianifmi in regimine Ecclefiae, quod Paftoribus adjungerent alios Doctores, & Rectores, quae humani commenti dicebat . . . deficit, etc.

himself and his people. And as, on a former occasion, it has been intimated that it is "very much a question" whether Smyth and his company would recognize my statement of their grounds of action "as correct and adequate," [37] I beg the reader particularly to observe, first, that I give that statement in *Smyth's own language,* even to the minutest jot and tittle of his spelling; and, second, that it is the *full summary* which he himself drew up of *the entire case which his book was designed to argue.* It is as follows: [38]

Our differences from the auncyent brethren of the Seperation:

1. Wee hould that the worſhip of the new teſtament properly ſo called is ſpirituall, proceeding originally from the hart : & that reading out of a booke (though a lawfull eccleſiaſtical action) is no part of ſpirituall worſhip, but rather the invention of the man of ſynne, it being ſubſtituted for a part of ſpirituall worſhip.
2. Wee hould that ſeeing propheſiing is a parte of ſpiritual worſhip : therefore in time of propheſijng it is vnlawfull to have the booke as a helpe before the eye.
3. wee hould that ſeeing ſinging a pſalme is a part of ſpirituall worſhip, therefore it is vnlawfull to have the booke before the eye in time of ſinginge a psalme.
4. wee hould that the Preſbytery of the church is vniforme : & that the triformed Preſbyterie conſiſting of three kinds of Elders, viz. Paſtors, Teachers, Rulers, is none of Gods Ordinance but mans devise. [39]
5. wee hold that all the Elders of the Church are Paſtors : and that lay Elders (ſo called) are Antichriſtian.
6. wee hold that in contributing to the Church Treaſurie, their ought to bee both a ſeparation from them that are without, & a ſanctification of the whole action by Prayer & Thankeſgiuing.

There is absolutely no solitary coeval witness to modify the drift of this testimony; apparently the first writer who alleges that anything other than this came in as an element, having written one hundred and thirty years after, and at the time freely confessed the inadequacy of his acquaintance with the

---

[37] I refer to the editorial of the Chicago *Standard* of 1 July, 1880. The New York *Examiner and Chronicle* of 19 Aug. 1880, fell into the same vein, saying: "Other questions are known to have been involved in producing the separation; but they do not exclude the change to Baptist views, which has been declared with great unanimity to be the primary cause." To which I now reply: (1) that the fact that the *complete* statement about to be given from Smyth's own pen makes no reference to any "Baptist views" does necessarily "exclude" them; and (2) that neither Smyth, nor his people, had any "Baptist views," at the date when the event now under consideration took place.

[38] *The Diferences of the Churches of the ſeperation. Contayning A deſcription of the Leitourgie and Miniſterie of the viſible Church Annexed: . . . Publiſhed, for the Satiſfaction of every true lover of the truth, eſpecially the Brethren of the Seperation that are doubtfull.* 2. *As alſo for the removing of an Vnjuſt Calumnie caſt vppon the Brethren of the Seperation of the ſecond Engliſh Church at Amſterdam.* 3. *Finally for the clearing of the truth, & the diſcovering of the myſterie of iniquitie yet further in the worſhip & offices of the Church. Divided into two parts:* (1) *Concerning the Leitourgie of the Church;* (2) *Concerning the Miniſterie of the Church. One of the Eldership. Another of the Deacons office whereto aperteineth the Treaſury,* etc. by John Smyth. [n. pl.] [n. d.] [1609.] [4°. pp. iv, 36.] [Bodleian. (Pamph. 6.)] p. v.

[39] Here, and in the following head (5), the divergence of Mr. Smyth from Barrowism in the direction of Brownism, is more marked than in previous cases to which reference has been made.

facts.[40] In the face of all this, to continue to affirm that the subject of baptism had anything to do with that cessation of communion between the first and second churches which took place in 1608, is not only to substitute the single unsupported conjecture of the fourth generation after for the uniform testimony of the time, but is to be wiser than that which was written by the man himself and his contemporaries. To sum all up into a single sentence, as Henry Ainsworth did, in 1613, this conflict, with its consequent cessation of fraternity, was caused by " M. Smyth in deed leaving the truth, and broaching his herefie againſt the tranflated fcripture." [41]

Not many months elapsed, however, before the active mind of this intrepid man did evolve that new view in regard to the ordinance above referred to, which, with its consequences, has made his name especially memorable; and the exact truth in regard to which I am now especially concerned to establish. We may perhaps most wisely reach the material of a sound conclusion as to the case in all its aspects, by answering the following three questions, viz.: When did this change of conviction take place? What were the modes of baptism then prevalent, and which of them did Smyth and his company probably make use of? and Did Mr. Smyth first rebaptize himself, and then administer the ordinance to his associates?

1. *When did this change of conviction take place?* We have already traced the history to the adoption by Mr. Smyth and apparently by the great body of his people, of those views which led to a cessation of fellowship with the "ancient" church; with the publication of the treatise intended to explain and justify that course — all of which seems to have taken place in the late spring or early summer of 1608;[42] and we have discovered down to this time no symptom of special interest in the subject of baptism, or of dissatisfaction on his part with his life-long position respecting it. But inertia once overcome,

---

[40] *Crosby* [1738] i; 92.

[41] *An Animadverſion to Mr. Richard Clyftons Advertiſement*, etc. Amsterdam, 1613. [4°. pp. viii, 138.] [B. M. (4103, d.)] p. 108.

[42] The difficulty of exactly determining the period in question is increased by the looseness with which books were sometimes dated in those days. Of course the *Paralleles*, etc. must have been sent to press while Mr. Smyth was still a Brownist, and before the arising of any difficulty between the "ancient" and second churches, yet its title-page bears clearly the imprint of "1609." On the other hand the preface of *The Character of the Beast*, etc. written *after* the full development of the Baptist change, concludes: " I end writing this 24 of March, 1608"; while the *Diferences*, etc., which bears no date, must have been published between them. After considerable thought I harmonize all by the theory that the *Paralleles* was sent to press early in 1608, but was — as I have noticed to be the fact in some other cases — wrongly dated; and that the 24th March 1608 is old style, which would make it the last day of that year, but by modern computation 24 Mar. [*i. e.* the 83d day of] 1609. Thus (especially as months very likely elapsed after the dating of the preface of *The Character*, etc. before its issue from the press) time enough is afforded for the entire succession of events; assigning the non-communion excitement, with the *Diferences*, etc. to the late spring or early summer, and the change of view on Baptism to the autumn or winter of 1608, followed by the *Character of the Beast*, etc. in the summer or fall of 1609. Clearly no great amount of time was lost, in any case.

progress becomes less difficult, and no doubt the sharp discussion which arose, on the one hand inclined these radicals to be hospitable toward further views which had always been under the ban of their former associates; and on the other, invited toward them the attention and persuasion of kindred minds which had already made wider departure from the Orthodoxy of the day. There were many Anabaptists — as they were then uniformly called — in Amsterdam; and it is very likely, though I do not know that the conjecture can be authenticated by evidence, that Hans de Ries or Lubbert Gerrits, or some other of these, with whom Smyth and his people were subsequently affiliated, may at this time have approached to leaven him with their peculiar views. Bradford indeed says "he was drawn away by some of the Dutch Anabaptists."[43] No long period, clearly, elapsed before, with or without their aid, Mr. Smyth was led to renounce his infant consecration, and to reconstruct his church upon the basis of a new adult baptism. This seems to have been fully accomplished during the closing months of 1608, being the first three months of 1609, by new style. But what I am chiefly anxious to do here is still further to make clear the fact that there was a distinct interval of time between it and the previous controversy which had called out the *Diferences of the Churches of the Separation*. Of this there remain at least six witnesses, as follows, viz.:

(1.) Richard Clyfton, having referred to the controversy about the Scriptures with its subsequent separation, goes on to say:[44]

After this, they diffolved their Church (which before was conioyned in the fellowfhip of the Gofpel & profeffion of the true fayth) & Mr. Smyth being Paftor thereof, gave over his office, as did alfo the Deacons, and devifed to enter a new communion by renouncing their former baptifme, and taking upon them another, of mans invention, etc.

(2.) Henry Ainsworth, after having dwelt at great length upon the cessation of fellowship and its causes, proceeds:[45]

Soon after this God ftroke him [Mr. Smyth] with blindnes, that he could no longer find the door of the Church out of which he was gone by fchifme, and which he had affaulted with error . . . And now as a man benummed in mynd, he cryeth out againft us, contrary to his former fayth and confeffion: Loe [*Character of the Beast*, etc. (Epistle)] *we proteft against them* (fayth he) *to bee a falfe Church, falfely conftituted in the baptifing of infants, and their own unbaptifed eftate*, etc.

(3.) Governor Bradford speaks distinctly to the same effect where he says:[46]

He first fell into some errors about the Scriptures, and so into some opposition with Mr.

---

[43] *Dialogue*, etc. in *Young*, 451.
[44] *Plea for Infants*, etc. v.
[45] *Defence*, etc. 3.
[46] *Dialogue*, etc. in *Young*, 450.

Johnson ... and the church there ... but *afterwards* was drawn away by some of the Dutch Anabaptists, etc.

(4.) Richard Bernard, after tracing in six steps Mr. Smyth's progress from the Establishment through Brownism, the sixth of which was his separation on the question of the Scriptures, goes on :[47]

Seauenthly, and laftly, if it prove the laft, He hath founded a new Church, hee hath (if you will beleeue him) recouered the true Baptifme, and the true matter and forme of a true Church, which now is onely to be found pure among a company of *Se-baptifts*, etc.

(5.) The author of *Ancient Truth Revived* . . . *or a true State of the antient Suffering Church of Chrift commonly (but falfely) called Brownifts*, etc., after making mention of the severance of Smyth and his friends from the fellowship of the "ancient" church, adds :[48]

Soon after Satan drew him to deny the Covenant preached to Abraham to be the Covenant of Grace, which led him to deny his Baptifm received in Infancy, etc.

(6.) Mr. Smyth himself testifies clearly on this point. Not having said one word about Baptism in his *Diferences*, in 1608, in his *Character of the Beast*, etc. "Printed 1609," he undertakes to meet the objection made against him of inconstancy in religion ; thus :[49]

to chandge a falfe Religion is commendable & to retaine a falfe Religion is damnable. For a man of a Turk to become a Iew, of a Iew to become a Papift, of a Papift to become a Proteftant are al commendable chandges, though they al of them befal one & the fame perfon in one yeere, nay, if it were in one month : So that not to chandg Religion is evil fimply : & therfor that we fhould fal from the profeffion of Puritanifme to Brownifme, & from Brown-ifme to true Chriftian baptifme, is not fimply evil or reprovable in it self, except it be proved that we have fallen from true religion : If wee therfor being formerly deceaved in the way of Pedobaptiftry, now doe embrace the truth in the true Chriftian Apoftolique baptifme : then let no man impute this as a fault vnto vs.

There being no suggestion of evidence, or even opinion, on the other side until more than one hundred years after, we may, in the light of these declarations, safely conclude that it was at some time in 1608, several months subsequent to the cessation of communion between the two churches, that Mr. Smyth led his flock forward to a dissolution of their old covenant, with reorganization on the basis of a new baptism.

2. *What modes of Baptism were then prevalent, and which mode did Smyth and his company, in all likelihood, make use of ?* This inquiry becomes the more needful from the very general assumption that at that time there, as at present

---

[47] *Plaine Euidences*, etc. 19.
[48] [B. M. (105. c. 49.)] p. 36.

[46] Bodleian, (Pamph. 7) p. iii. This book is not in the B. M. library.

among us, the two methods of sprinkling and of immersion alone prevailed; with the result that all descriptive and other language which it would hardly be natural to apply to the former, has been taken as of course implying the latter.[50] It will be further well if we can obtain the means of determining whether the statement often made that infant baptism at this time in England was uniformly administered by immersion, with the inference that therefore the adoption of that form by the Baptists for adults would not be likely to call forth special remark,[51] stands upon any sufficient basis of fact.

It is conceded, even by those who are most earnest in the claim that immersion was the earliest form of administering Christian baptism, that it was soon dispensed with in exceptional cases;[52] while it is matter of undoubted history that within little more than one hundred years subsequent to the death of the last of the Apostles, Novatian, being sick, "was baptized by affusion in the bed on which he lay;"[53] and that, soon after, the frequency of like cases led Magnus to put to Cyprian, Bishop of Carthage, the question whether such procedure were valid. We have the very words of his reply:[54]

Quaesisti etiam, fili carissime, quid mihi de illis videatur, qui in infirmitate et languore gratiam Dei consequuntur, an habendi sint legitimi christiani eo, quod aqua salutari non loti sint, sed perfusi.

... Nos quantum concipit mediocritas nostra aestimamus, in nullo mutilari et debilitari posse beneficia divina, nec minus aliquid illic posse contingere, ubi plena et tota fide et dantis et sumentis accipitur, quod de divinis muneribus hauritur.

[Then, after citing Ezek. xxxvi: 25, 26; Numbers xix: 8, 12, 13; viii: 5-7 and xix: 9.

You have asked also, dearest son, what I thought of those who obtain God's grace in sickness and weakness; whether they are to be accounted legitimate Christians, for that they are not washed, but sprinkled, with the saving water.

... As far as my poor understanding conceives it, I think that the divine benefits can in no respect be mutilated and weakened; nor can anything less occur in that case, where, with full and entire faith both of the giver and receiver, is accepted what is drawn from the divine gifts.

---

[50] *E. g.* "The definition of baptism in Helwys's Confession, published in 1611, viz.: '*washing* with water,' instead of proving affusion, we think very good Baptist [*i. e.* immersionist] testimony." *Examiner and Chronicle*, 19 Aug. 1880. See also a learned article by Dr. Heman Lincoln, Prof. of Eccl. Hist. at Newton Theo. Sem. in the *Watchman and Reflector*, 14 Oct. 1880.

[51] So well informed a man as Dr. Evans — who seems to have been almost alone among his English Baptist brethren of this generation in taking much pains to get at the real *facts* of the early history of the Baptists in that country — says [*Early English Baptists*, etc. i: 203 *note*]: "The all but universal practice of immersion in the English Church rendered the discussion of the mode unnecessary." It is curious — I may as well add here as anywhere — to observe with what *sang-froid* this writer now and again refers in his notes to books which he was aware advocated views lying athwart other views to which he refers, as works which "we have not seen;" when he must have known that a few shillings, and a little trouble, would take him to the British Museum, or the Bodleian, or to York Minster, where he could hardly fail to " see" them.

[52] Vide Taylor's *General Baptists*, etc. 1: 61.

[53] "ἐν αὐτῇ τῇ κλίνῃ ᾗ ἔκειτο περιχυθείς." *Letter of Cornelius to Fabius. Eusebius, Eccl. Hist.* VI: xliii.

[54] *Epistola* LXIX. [Tauchnitz ed.] 193.

he goes on]: unde apparet, adspersionem quoque aquae instar salutaris lavacri obtinere, et quando haec in ecclesia fiunt, ubi sit et accipientis et dantis fides integra, stare omnia et consummari ac perfici posse maiestate Domini et fidei veritate.

Whence it appears that the sprinkling also of water prevails equally with the washing of salvation; and that when this is done in the church, where the faith both of receiver and giver is sound, all things hold and may be consummated and perfected by the majesty of the Lord, and by the truth of faith.

By the fifth century there is evidence that in France affusion had come into at least occasional use as the mode of baptism for persons in health.[55] In the twelfth century sprinkling, pouring and immersion coexisted in Italy;[56] and, in 1311, Clement V. sanctioned the action of the second Council of Ravenna making ["sub trina aspersione vel immersione"] sprinkling or immersion optional.[57] In England a Roman Catholic historian judges that while the Anglo-Saxon Church enjoined immersion for infants, in the case of adults it was accustomed to administer "by affusion upon the head."[58] In the fifteenth century Lyndewood says that, where the child is not strong enough to be immersed, or the priest is too feeble to immerse it, baptism may be properly done ["per modum effusionis vel aspersionis"] by pouring or sprinkling.[59] The first Prayer-Book of the Reformation — that of Edward VI. of 1549 — ordained: "first dypping the ryghtsyde: Seconde the left syde: The thyrde tyme dippyng the face towarde the fonte: So it be discretly and warely done," but it is added: "if the childe be weake, it shall suffice to poure water vpon it, etc."[60] This was modified in the second book of Edward VI. of 1552, by leaving out the trine immersion, but retaining the same provision in the case of danger of harm from even the single dipping.[61]

In 1536 Calvin published at Basle the first edition of his *Institutes of the Christian Religion*, in which on this subject he said:[62]

---

[55] *Gennadius of Marseilles* says the candidate for baptism is "either wetted with the water, or else plunged into it." *De Eccl. Dogmatibus*, etc. c. 74, as cited by *Wall*, ii: 357.

[56] *Thomas Aquinas*, [Q. lxvi. Art. 7] as cited by *Wall*, ii: 357. So Bunsen says (*Hyppolytus and his Age*, etc. (1854) ii: 121] "The Western Church evidently commenced her career, under the guidance of Rome, with more freedom of thought. She abolished, together with adult baptism, its symbol, immersion, and introduced sprinkling in its stead."

[57] *Labbe*, R. XI.

[58] Very Rev. Canon Flanagan, *History of the Church in Eng.*, etc. i: 178.

[59] *Provinciale*, etc. 242. There is a curious passage in Tyndall's *Obedience of a Christian Man*, etc.

(1528) which refers to this exceptional practice, where he is rebuking the spiritual ignorance of the common people [*Doctrinal Treatises*, (Parker Soc. ed. 1848,) 277]:

Behold how narrowly the people look on the ceremony. If aught be left out, or if the child be not altogether dipt in the water; or if, because the child is sick, the priest dare not plunge him into the water, but pour water on his head, how tremble they! how quake they! "How say ye, Sir John" (say they) "is this child christened enough? Hath it his full christendom?" They believe verily that the child is not christened.

[60] Fol. CXV̄J.

[61] Signature X. 2 (iii).

[62] *Institutio Christianae Religionis*, etc. Lib. IV. cap. xv, secs. 19, 20.

Cæterum mergatur ne totus qui tingitur, idque ter an femel, an infufa tantum aqua afpergatur, minimum refert: fed id pro regionum diuerfitate Ecclefiis liberum effe debet ... Vbi inualuit opinio, perditos effe omnes quibus aqua tingi non contigit, noftra conditio deterior eft quam veteris populi, qua fi reftrictior effet Dei gratia quam fub Lege.

Whether the person baptized is to be wholly immersed, and that whether once or thrice, or whether he is only to be sprinkled with water, is not of the least consequence: churches should be at liberty to adopt either according to the diversity of climates ... When the opinion prevails that all are lost who happen not to be dipped in water, our condition becomes worse than that of God's ancient people; as if His grace were more restrained than under the Law.

Under the rubric as it stood (and indeed still stands) two causes during Elizabeth's reign have been supposed to have swayed the flexible practice of the English Church from immersion toward sprinkling. One, the strong preference often had by parents — especially of that wealthier and more cultured class which so much sets the fashion for the humbler sort — for sprinkling, or pouring, over dipping, because they enjoyed neither the stripping their children naked of the fine garments prepared for their christening, nor the affrighted screams with which the little ones were apt to receive immersion;[63] the other, the fact that when those English divines who during bloody Mary's reign had taken shelter in Germany and Switzerland, came back, they brought with them as to this subject a preference for Calvin's more liberal theory and practice.[64] In the second year of Elizabeth, we find Thomas Becon adding his influence to the movement, thus:[65]

Chrift commanded to baptize all men; but he left the manner of baptizing free to his Church, whether they would wafh the whole body, or fome part thereof. Moreover, as all the people of the Jews was counted to be fprinkled with the blood of the covenant, becaufe it was accuftomed to be fprinkled upon all, when notwithftanding not their whole bodies, but fome part of them was imbrued with the blood; fo likewife a man or an infant is taken to be wholly baptized, dipped and cleanfed, when fome one member only is overflowed with water, dipped or cleanfed. For this lawifh [66] fprinkling was a figure of the blood of Chrift, wherewith the

---

[63] Vide *Wall*, ii: 365.
[64] Calvin's own practice was pouring. His Genevan Liturgy [*Catechismus Genevensis*, etc. (Niemeyer's *Collectio Confessionum*, etc. 1840), 183] prescribes the form to be: [Tum in eum *aquam* Baptifmi minifter *effundit*, inquiens, etc.] "Then the minifter *pours water on the infant*, saying, etc." About the same time we find Bullinger, at Zurich, using such language as the following [*Fiftie Godlie and Learned Sermons*, etc. (ed. 1587) p. 1040], viz.:
There is contention alfo about this: whether once or thrife hee that is baptifed, ought to bee dipped, or fprinckeled with water. Truely the Apostles haue not curioufly commaunded anything in this behalfe. So that *it is free either to fprinckle or to dip*. Sprinckling feemeth to haue been vfed of the old Fathers: for honefty and fhamefaftenefse forbiddeth to vncover the body; and also the (wenke) ftate of Iufants for the moft part, can not away with dipping; since fprinkling alfo doeth as much as dipping. And it ftandeth in the choyce of him that miniftreth baptifme, to fprinckle him either once or thrice, after the cuftome of the Church, whereof hee is minifter.

[65] *A new Catechifme, fette forth Dialogewife*, etc. [Parker Soc. ed. 1844], 227.

[66] "Lawish sprinkling" = that sprinkling which was prescribed and practiced under the law.

confciences are fprinkled, and of our baptifm. Furthermore, feeing that the virtue and power of cleanfing the minds cometh not from the water, it is all one matter, whether the whole body, or fome part thereof, as the head, be wafhed. It is therefore fufficient if the fignification of fpiritual baptifm be obferved.

That to "baptize" fignifieth not to plunge the whole man into the water, it may eafily be gathered both of St. Mark's and St. Luke's gofpel, where we read thus: [67] *Reverfi a foro non comedunt nifi prius baptizati;* that is, "The Pharifees, when they come home from the market, eat not, except they firft be baptized" — that is to fay, wafh their hands. Again: [68] *Mirabatur Pharifaeus quod Chriftus non baptizatus accumbat menfae;* that is: "The Pharifee marveled that Chrift was not baptized," that is to fay, wafhed not his hands, "before he fat down at the table."

Opinions differ, testimony is not uniform, and practice may have varied in different parts of the kingdom, but I see no sufficient reason to doubt the conclusion of W. Walker, a very careful writer who gave large attention to the subject but little more than two generations after,[69] that, during the later half of the seventeenth century pouring, or sprinkling, "became the more general," as when he wrote, it was "almoft the only way of Baptizing" in England.

J. Watts, who wrote like a man of learning and wide research, more than twenty years before Walker, summing up some thirty pages of close historical review, said if immersion were the original baptism it had given place to sprinkling and aspersion:[70] "which have wholly fupplanted it . . . and fo got away the blefling from it, to be *the only approved and practifed way* in the centuries fucceeding." Mr. Wall, who published a little later, and who received from Oxford the complimentary degree of D.D. for the eminent ability of his work, says:[71]

The Inclination of the People, back'd with thefe authorities,[72] carried the Practice againft the Rubric; which ftill requir'd Dipping, except in Cafe of Weaknefs. So that *in the later Times of Queen Elizabeth, and during the Reigns of King James and of King Charles I. very few Children were dipt in the Font.*

It was natural that the Reformed Churches should feel the influence of Calvin's judgment, while Zwingli, in his Confession of Faith to Charles V. (1530) said:[73]

---

[67] Mark vii: 4.
[68] Luke xi: 38.
[69] W. Walker, *The Doctrine of Baptifms,* etc. (1678). 147.
[70] J. Watts, *A Scribe, Pharisee, Hypocrite, and his Letter anfwered,* etc. 63.
[71] W. Wall, *The Hiftory of Infant Baptifm,* etc. (1720) ii: 366.
[72] He had just cited Musculus [*Loci Communi de Baptifmo,* etc. 431]: "As for Dipping of the Infant; we judge that not fo neceffary, but that it is free for the Church to baptize either by Dipping or Sprinkling;" and Dr. Whitaker, Regius Prof. at Cambridge [*Praelectiones de Sacr. de Bap.* etc. Q. 1. c. 2]: "in the cafe of Infants and fickly People, I think fprinkling fufficient."
[73] *Ad Carolum Rom. Imp. Fidei II. Zuinglii Ratio* [Niemeyer], 26.

Cum baptizamur, abluitur corpus mundifsimo elemento: fed hoc fignificatur, gratia divinae bonitatis in Ecclefiae et populi Dei coetum allectos effe, in quo candide fit ac pure vivendum, etc.	When we are baptized, the body is *washed* in the purest element; but by this is signified that through the riches of divine mercy we are gathered in to the company of the church and people of God, in which one should live a clean and holy life.

This symbolism, of washing with water as the token of that spiritual cleansing properly belonging to entrance upon Church life, thenceforward shows itself in many of the Reformed Confessions, and naturally appears to have been connected especially with affusion, or the method of baptism by pouring and rubbing water upon the recipient. Thus the Later Confession of Helvetia (1566) in this manner speaks:[74]

Ideoque baptifamur, id eft, abluimur, aut afpergimur aqua vifibili. Aqua enim fordes mundat, deficientia et aeftuantia recreat, et refrigerat corpora. Gratia vero Dei haec animabus praeftat, et quidem invifibiliter vel fpiritualiter.	And therefore are we baptized, that is, *washed and sprinkled* with visible water. For the water maketh clean that which is filthy, and refresheth and cooleth the bodies that fail and faint. And the grace of God dealeth in like manner with the soul; and that invisibly and spiritually.

In the same year the Belgic Confession used the following language as to the same subject, viz.:[75]

Sicut enim aqua in nos effufa et fuper corpus baptizati eminens ipfumque irrigans, fordes corporis abluit: fic et Sanguis Chrifti animam abluens, a peccatis illum emundat, nofque filios irae in filios Dei regenerat . . . Neque tamen hic Baptifmus eo duntaxat momento prodeft, quo aqua nobis inhaeret, aut quo ea tingimur: fed per totum vitae noftrae tempus.	For as water, *being poured upon us,* and appearing on the body of him that is baptized, moistening the same, doth wash away the filthiness of the body; so the blood of Christ, washing the soul, doth cleanse it from sin, and doth make us, which before were the children of wrath, the sons of God . . . Neither doth this baptism profit us only at that moment *when the water resteth upon us, and when we are moistened with it;* but it is available throughout the whole time of our life.

In 1573 the Confession of Bohemia defined baptism as [ablutio hominis per aquam cum invocatione nominis Sacrofanctae Trinitatis, etc.][76] "the *washing of the candidate with water* in the name of the holy Trinity." It is added:[77] "that washing is used both to signify, and to witness, a spiritual washing and inward cleansing of the Holy Ghost, from the disease of hereditary sin, and from other sins, etc."

In entire accord with this we find the French Churches prescribing that the

---

[74] *Confeffio Helvetica pofterior.* Niemeyer, 517.
[75] *Conf. Belg. Ibid.* 384. [76] *Conf. Bohem. Ibid.* 840.
[77] *Harmony of Protestant Confessions,* etc. (1844), 304.

water be *poured upon* the person to be baptized,[78] and the Waldenses [Les Eglises Vaudoises] describing baptism [c'est à dire en noftre langage, lavement d'eau, ou de fleuve, ou de fontaine][79] as, "the *washing with water*, either that of a river, or a fountain, in the name of the Father," etc. The Dutch Established Churches were an offshoot of the Lutheran side of the Reformation. But the Heidelberg Catechism (1563) lays an entirely similar stress upon that symbolism of the rite which implies its administration by affusion. Thus [*Question* lxix] :[80]

Q. Wie wirst du in der heiligen Taufe erinnert und versichert, dasz das einige Opfer Christi am Kreuz dir zu gut komme?

A. Also, dasz Christus dieses auszerliche Wasserbad eingesetzt, und dabei verheiszen hat, dasz ich so gewisz mit seinem Blut und Geist von der Unreinigkeit meiner Seele, das ist, allen meinen Sünden gewaschen sei, so gewisz ich auszerlich mit dem Wasser, welches die Unsauberkeit des Leibes pflegt hinzunehmen, gewaschen bin.

Q. How is it signified and sealed unto thee in Holy Baptism, that thou hast part in the one sacrifice of Christ on the cross?

A. Thus: that Christ has appointed this outward *washing* with water, and has joined therewith this promise, that I am washed with His blood and Spirit from the pollution of my soul, that is, from all my sins, as certainly *as I am washed outwardly with water, whereby commonly the filthiness of the body is taken away.*

What the practice in Holland actually was under this Catechism will be made sure from the Expositions of that symbol by J. Bastingius and P. de Witte. The former says :[81]

The ceremony, or rite, is declared by *wafhing or fprinckling with water*, in that the bodie of him that is baptized, is fprinckled with this water. For this is the ende why water is vfed, not to be idle, but to be applied to the body, to fprinkle it or to wafh it, according to the commandment of Christ: Hereof the Apoftle defineth Baptifme: the wafhing of water by the worde, etc.

The latter says :[82]

Q. How is it [Baptism] *done in thefe Countreys?*

A. With fprinkling; as the word Baptifme may alfo be taken for that, Mark vii: 4 *wafhings of beds*, (Baptifmes as in the Greek), Heb. ix: 10.

Q. Ought we not again to bring in dipping, as the Mufcowites and others do?

A. It is not neceffary; becaufe *wafhing is done with fprinkling* as well as by dipping, etc.

We have moreover the testimony of a traveler, taken on the spot a few

---

[78] Quick, *Synodicon in Gallia Reformata*, etc. (1692), ii : 453.

[79] Jean Leger, *Hiftoire Generale des Eglifes Evangeliques des Vallees de Piemont*, etc. (1669) 65.

[80] I quote from the later German and English versions as given authentically in the *Tercentenary Edition* (1863), by the German Reformed Church in this country, p. 201.

[81] *An Expofition or Commentarie upon the Catechifme of Chriftian religion which is taught in the Scholes and Churches of the Lowe Countries*, etc. (1593) p. 138, verso.

[82] *Catechizing upon the Heidelbergh Catechifme*, etc. *publifhed after Precedent Infpection and Approbation of the Rev. Claffis of Hoorn*, etc., *and now after the Sixtienth Impreffion tranflated for the Englifh Reformed Congregation in Amfterdam*, etc. p. 514.

years later. Sir William Brereton describes a baptism which he witnessed in Amsterdam in 1634, by which time, in that unaltering land, no great change, it is fair to think, had modified the Dutch custom of the early part of the same generation : [83]

The minister here baptized after sermon fourteen children; the water not sprinkled upon their faces, but the predicant doth pull back the cloth and dressing on the head, so that all the skull of the child's head is bare, and holding the face downwards, he is sufficiently prodigal of water, *pouring divers handfuls upon the child's head*, and holding his hand on the child's head, *rubbing the same during all the time that he is pronouncing the words of baptism*, which, as I conceived,[84] were equivalent to those of ours : — "I baptize thee in the name of the Father, Son, etc." using as long a speech whilst he held the child in his arms, as our [English] ministers do. I observed diligently, and he used not the sign of the cross, which all the Dutch churches reject. Here were no god-fathers; those that brought and carried the children gave the name unto the predicant, and all those were women that held and brought the children.

There was a Dutch Church in London which published the *Corpus Difciplinae*, or the Body of Discipline, used in the Reformed Churches of Holland, from which I take the following, as showing the rule they recognized, viz. : [85]

As for fprinkling once or three times, we hold it indifferent . . . Sprinkling with water teacheth us . . . the *wafhing away* of our sins by Jefus Christ . . . As *water being poured upon us*, and being feen and fprinkled upon the body of him that is baptized, *doth wafh away the filthinefs of the body*, fo likewife the blood of Christ by the operation of the Holy Ghoft inwardly worketh the fame in the foul.

So far as the Established Reformed Churches of Holland, and the French (Walloon) Churches existing there, are concerned — together making the great majority of all — it is now clear that the ordinance of baptism was administered by pouring, accompanied with such friction of the subject of it as should suggest that washing from the filth of the flesh, which furnished the symbolism especially emphasized in their creeds. There were also some Anabaptists and Mennonites in the Low Countries at the beginning of the seventeenth century, whose practice in this regard we need to investigate, as well.

I shall perhaps surprise some of my readers — but not more than the discovery astonished myself — when I say that the Anabaptists do not appear to have begun with baptism by immersion. Hoornbeek (1653) seems to be one of the most careful and comparatively unprejudiced writers upon the Anabaptistic movement of his time. He lays down five points as peculiar to them in Holland — from which insistence on immersion is noticeably omitted — viz. : [86]

---

[83] *Travels, etc. Cheetham Soc. Pub.* p. 64.
[84] He did not understand Dutch well enough to be sure.
[85] *Corpus Difciplinae*, etc. (1645) [B. M. (E. 313. [15.])], 7, 12, 63.
[86] *Summa Controverf. Relig.* etc. (ed. 1658), 359.

Apud nos vulgo noti funt ex quinque articulis: oppugnati paedobaptifmi, erroris primarii, & apud illos communiſſimi; defenſi anabaptifmi; negatæ Chriſti ex Matris fubſtantia incarnationis; interdicti ipſis omnis generis juramenti; & officii Magiſtratus.

With us they are commonly known by five tenets, viz.: (1) they oppose infant baptism, their fundamental error, shared by all; (2) they insist upon rebaptism; (3) they deny that Christ took his flesh from his mother; (4) they forbid their members to take oath, or (5) to hold the magistrate's office.

Lambertus Hortensius (1548)[87] and Guy de Bres (1565)[88] are two of the earliest and most careful historians of the origin and progress of Anabaptism, and their statements fully accord with this summary which Hoornbeek gives. I have in my possession a curious confirmation — of date 1579 — of the substantial accuracy of this *résumé*. It is entitled [*Een Nieu Liedeken*, etc.][89] "A New Song, made by two Friends sacrificed in London, in the year 1575," etc. These "two Friends" were John Pieters and Henry Terwoort, the protomartyrs under Elizabeth. It relates how they were summoned to St. Paul's Church and questioned, and their own account of the interview is (partly) this, viz.:

Daer waren vergaert, feer veel vermaert	There were gathered, very many celebrated
Leeraers hooghe gheacht	Professors highly esteemed
Den Biſſchof als die ſtercke	The Bishop as the strong one
En ander volck by macht.	And other people of consideration.
Vier vraghen fy voorſtelden	They proposed four questions
Deerſte van waer hy quam	The first from where He came
Van Chriſto fy vertelden	From Christ they said
Off hy zijn vleefch aen nam	If he had taken his flesh
Van Maria faen wy en verſlaen	From Mary sweet; we do not understand it
So niet ghelijck ghy fegt	As you say it.
Noch met vraghen fy heur quelden:	Still with questions they plagued them:
Is dan tfweeren onrecht.	Is then taking an oath a crime?
Dees antwoorde wilt hooren	Listen to this answer
Die was dander ghelijck	It was like unto the other
Noch ſtelden fy haer vooren	They also propounded to them:
Mach een Chriſten publijck	May a Christian publicly
Sijn kinderen fnel doen doopen wel	Cause his children to be baptized quickly
Segt ons trechte bediet	Give us the right interpretation?
Sy fpraken fonder verſtooren	They replied, without anger,
Wy en hebbens ghelefen niet.	We have not read it.
Noch vraechden fy na defen	Yet after this they asked
Vermach een Chriſten ledt	Is a Christian allowed
Een ouerheyt te wefen	To be a magistrate
En te bedienen net	And to serve as such?
En falich zijn; verſtaet wel mijn	And will he be saved; understand me well,
Segt ons dat recht befcheyt.	Give us the right explanation of this.

---

[87] *Tumultuum Anabaptiſtarum*, etc. 11.
[88] *La Racine Source et Fondement des Anabaptiſtes ou Rebaptiſez de noſtre Temps*, etc. *passim*.

[89] *Van Gheboden*, etc. *hier achter is noch by ghenoecht een Liedeken van ii Vrienden opgeoffert te Lonnen in Enghelant. Int iaer M.D.LXXV.* (1579) 16°, p. 163.

[19]

From the confessions involved in the chaos of these rude stanzas it is easy to see — what indeed is made evident by the histories of the time [97] — that these poor Flemings were burned for insisting on the "five points" above named.

If, now, it were true, as it has been common in some quarters to assert, that immersion were the universal method of administering the rite of Baptism, when, near the close of the first quarter of the sixteenth century, Stork and Muncer laid the foundations of Anabaptism, the inferences would be allowable: (1) that the new sect baptized in the common way; and (2) that, so doing, no reference would be natural to their practice in that respect either in their own creed, or in the popular objections first raised against them. We have seen, however, that the reverse was the fact, and that the method of baptizing then nearly universal was by pouring, or sprinkling.[91] And this fact renders it inevitable that had the Anabaptists begun by laying down the law that dipping is the only valid baptism, that law would have found a place in the summary of their belief, while their practice under it must have provoked the dissent of those who followed a different way. Neither being true, the conclusion seems inevitable that they administered baptism, as others around them did, by affusion.

This quite agrees with Robert Baylie's statement, in 1647:[92]

Among the old Anabaptiſts, or thoſe over ſea to this day ſo far as I can learn by their writs [writings] or any relation that has yet come to my ears, the queſtion of dipping and ſprinkling came never upon the Table. As I take it, they dip none, but all whom they baptize they ſprinkle in the same manner as is our cuſtome.

Here, again, I have stumbled upon the acquisition of what seems to me a strong confirmatory proof of the view which I take. It is an ancient Dutch version of Lambertus Hortensius,[93] containing illustrations. Over against the statement which this author makes in regard to the original Anabaptist baptism — which is the following, viz.:[94] [*et inter iſta ſeditionis capita celebriora Muntzeri erat nouus baptiſmus in libera eccleſia, quem præclarus ille toto orbe refragante tueri uoluit*] "and among the chief tenets of the sedition of Munzer, was

---

[90] See Strype, *Annals*, etc. ii (i): 564; Fuller, *Church History*, etc. iv: 390; Collier, *Eccl. Hist. Great Brit.* vi: 543; Evans, *Ear. Eng. Bap.* i: 151-165. See the writ for their execution in *Rymer. Foed.* XV. 740, and *Wilkins*, iv: 281.

[91] We have seen that the Romish Church had abandoned Immersion, and that the then newly forming Reformed Churches neither believed nor practiced it, but sprinkled or poured.

[92] *Anabaptiſm the True Fountain*, etc. 163.

[93] See note 87, *ante*. There is also in the library of the British Museum the first edition [as I suppose] of [Catrou's] *Hiſtoire des Anabaptiſtes; contenant leur Doctrine, les Diverſes Opinions, qui les diviſent en pluſieurs Sects; les Troubles, qu'ils ont cauſez, et enfin, tout ce qui ſ'eſt paſſé de plus conſiderable à leur egard, depuis l'an 1521 juſques à preſent.* Amsterdam, 1699. 12°. [B. M. (4139. c.)] which contains the same engraving, or a close copy thereof.

[94] p. 9.

that of a new baptism into a free Church, which that notorious man desired, in the face of all opposition, to promote " — is placed the engraving which I have had fac-similed for these pages. The "new baptism" was that re-baptism, as a believer, which was required of all who had been baptized in infancy. And the manner of it is shown to be *by affusion*. Not daring in the beginning to rouse popular opposition by any public re-administration of the rite, the service took place in a private house, as is shown by the bed on one side of the chamber; and the candidates kneeled before the dispenser, who lifted water in his hands, and let it fall upon their heads. I do not presume that this picture photographs any actual scene; but I do regard it as most unlikely that such a pictorial adjunct of so ancient a history would go to the length of violent and — as it would have been, were it untrue — offensive misrepresentation of a transaction which must have been well

known in its character, and was so vital to these people as to have given them their popular designation.

Whatever may have been the fact about this, and however some of the many minor subdivisions of the Anabaptist body[95] may have subsequently modified

---

[95] *De Bres* declares that these subdivisions soon became numerous. He says [p. 66]: Neantmoins afin de n'estre trop long, & de peur d'ennuyer les lecteurs de tant de diuersitez de sectes ie

their practice in this respect,[96] there is fortunately evidence that none of the Anabaptists in Holland baptized by immersion down to the year 1619. Without seeking to multiply citations, it will be sufficient to note : —

(1) the fact that — as we shall see directly — when in 1619 the *Collegianten* arose at Rynsburg, it is clear that they proceeded to difference themselves from all previous rejecters of infant baptism in Holland, by introducing dipping, or immersion ;

(2) the fact that Dr. Muller, the distinguished antiquary, himself a Dutch Mennonite, declared that previous to 1619[97] "the Waterlanders, nor any other of the various parties of the Netherland *Doopsgezinden* [Baptists], practiced at any time baptism by immersion ;" and

(3) the fact that Dr. J. G. de Hoop Scheffer, a learned professor at the present time in the Mennonite College at Amsterdam, and the man of all others who has studied the question with most advantage of culture and position, declares that[98] "the Collegianten (1619) were the first persons who practiced immersion in the Netherlands."

The Mennonites (proper) remain. But it was their habit to baptize by affusion ; as to that rite differing from the Reformed only [*sed neutiquam infantes*][99] in declining to baptize infants. Hermann Schyn, their faithful historian, devotes several pages to this subject. After stating several reasons which led them to reject immersion he concludes :[100]

---

n'en nōmeray feulemēt q̄ quinze de noms. En premier lieu il y a Thomas Muncer auec sa bande. Puis apres il y a les Anabaptiſtes Apoſtoliq̃s en ſecond lieu. Les Anabaptiſtes ſpirituels ſeparez du mōde. Les Anabaptiſtes faincts & ſans pechez, ce font les Parfaicts. Les Anabapſtles faiſons ſilence. Les Anabaptiſtes Pnans, & ſe ſians du tout en Dieu, reiettans tous moyens ordinaires. Les Anabaptiſtes Enthuſiaſtiques. Les gros Anabaptiſtes libres. Des freres Huttites. Des Anabaptiſtes Auguſtins. Des glorieux & triomphans Anabaptiſtes de Munſtre, de Melchior Hoffman, & les Meherlandrs. Et finalement des Mennonites de noſtre temps, & des Franiques, leſquels ſe font diuiſez depuis peu de iours. Ne voila pas biē creu & multiplié en ſi peu de tēps ?

[96] Rev. H. S. Burrage, editor of the *Zion's Advocate*, a Baptist journal published in Portland, Me. — who has made a special study of these questions — in an article on " Early English and American Baptists" published in the *Independent* of 21 Oct. 1880, says that as early as April, 1525, Wolfgang Uliman was immersed by Conrad Grebel in the Rhine at Schaffhausen. He adds that others were immersed a little later, in the Sitter river. This is cited from the diary of Kessler, of St. Gall. Mr. R. Barclay in his *Inner Life of the*

Relig. Socs. of the Commonwealth, etc. refers, as I suppose, to the same case [p. 75], saying: " From J. Kessler's *Sabbata*, a MS. printed by the Historical Society at St. Gallen, Switzerland, it appears that Uliman, afterwards a teacher in the Church of Anabaptists at St. Gallen, was dipt," apparently citing in proof Cornelius's *Geschichte des Munsterischen Aufruhrs*, ii: 32, 33, 36, 37, 64, which I have as yet failed to procure. Mr. Barclay adds that "the Swiss Unitarian Baptists sought a refuge in Poland, and, in 1550, the rite of immersion was practised in Poland."

[97] See his testimony in *Evans*, i : 223.
[98] See his testimony in *Barclay*, 75.
[99] Confession prepared by Hans de Ries and Lubbert Gerrits : *Article* xxxi. Schyn, *Historia Mennonitarum*, etc. i : 208.
[100] *Historia Mennonitarum*, etc. ii : 35-38. *Barclay* [83] says :

The Mennonites strongly condemned infant baptism and made use of adult baptism. It was administered by pouring water on the head of the person received, etc.

Quare plurimae noſtrae Eccleſiae Baptiſmum folummodo per effuſionem aquae in caput baptizandi adminiſtrant; certiſſime credentes quod non aquae multitudo, etſi eſſet totius Oceani, ſufficere poſſit ad noſtrorum peccatorum ablutionem, ſi baptiſmus non infucata fide & vera reſipiſcentia a nobis recipiatur.

Wherefore nearly all of our Churches administer baptism only by pouring water upon the head of the candidate; most surely believing that it is not the quantity of water — were it even the whole ocean — which can avail for the cleansing of our sins; unless our baptism is received by us with a genuine faith and a true repentance.

It is needful here still further to establish the fact that it was not until in 1619, that the *Collegianten*, one branch of the rejecters of infant baptism in Holland, did introduce immersion into that country; because as that date, although ten years subsequent to Smyth's se-baptism, was more than twenty previous to the rise of the Baptist controversy in England, confusion and misunderstanding have arisen in regard to it.[101] As to this the testimony of Brandt will be ample and conclusive. After describing, under date of A.D. 1619, their origin, he says:[102]

> From the place of their meeting they came to be called *Rynſburgers*; and from their way of holding forth, *Prophets*. They were afterwards ſtiled *Collegiants* [Collegianten], from the colleges or ſocieties which they eſtabliſhed in all places, where they could make a party. Having fixed their ſeparate meeting at Rynſburg, they likewiſe celebrated the Lords Supper together, and *began to advance the notion of dipping or plunging*, as the manner was among the Primitive Christians in the hot countries of the East. Thus became the *Plunging-baptiſm*, as they called it, in practice among them. They prevailed with some to ſuffer themſelves to be thus dipped all over in the very Tan-pits. They alſo uſed this kind of *plunging* with people, who, upon their own confeſſion, had been before baptized by the Anabaptiſts, in their old age. They rejected Infant-baptism, as well as the Anabaptiſts; and with them maintained that no Chriſtian ought to bear the office of a Magiſtrate, or to wage war.

One further subject requires mention before we are prepared to sum up the conclusions of this brief historical review.

Subsequent to the earliest introduction of the gospel to savage peoples, and after Christianity had had a few generations in which to settle down to its work, it became the theory in all branches of the Church — since it is clear that, whatever were the primitive practice, all then believed and thoroughly practised infant baptism — that there would be no adult candidates for the

---

[101] Thus the *Examiner and Chronicle*, of 19 Aug. 1880, says, speaking of the date of the organization of Smyth's church: "it is well known that while some of the Mennonites practiſed affuſion, many of them were immerſed" — citing *Mosheim* in proof. But Mosheim published his *Inſtitutiones* more than one hundred and fifty years ago, and the world has learned much since then as to ecclesiastical history. The remark would have been true if referred to the date of the organization of Spilsbury's Church in England, which was after 1619, but it is in error — as has been shown — as it stands.

[102] Gerard Brandt, *History of the Reformation in the Low Countries*, etc. [original, in Low Dutch, 1671, English translation, 1723] (ed. 1723) iv: 56. Compare Jan Wagenaar, *Amsterdam*, etc. (1765) ii: 204-206.

ordinance. Hence no provision appears in the ancient liturgies for any other than infant baptism. It was not until 1645 that, at the third Synod of Charenton, the Reformed Church of France made such provision,[103] nor until the revision of 1661 that the English Prayer-Book recognized such administration by the insertion of a form for the "Public Baptiſm of ſuch as are of Riper Years," which — says the Preface — "by yᵉ growth of Anabaptiſm,[104] through yᵉ Licentiouſneſs of yᵉ late Times crept in amongſt us, is now become neceſſary; and may be allwaies uſefull, for yᵉ baptizing of Natives in our Plantations, and others converted to yᵉ Faith."[105] Nor would the fonts of the 16th and 17th centuries, while large enough for the immersion of a new-born infant, have answered the same purpose for full-grown men and women.[106] I take it, then, that on those rare occasions of waifs from distant heathenism, and the like, when the ordinance needed to be administered to full-grown converts, they must have been sprinkled, or resort was had to a stream, or pool. And among those affusing Reformed Churches which laid stress upon the symbolism of washing off the filth of the flesh, as prefiguring that inward and spiritual cleansing which should fit the soul for its new relations, it would seem to be almost inevitable that the method of procedure adopted would be for the administrator and the candidate to wade in together until they reached a depth sufficient to enable the minister without much stooping to reach the surface with his hands, and for him then, with them, to lift and pour water upon the neophyte's head and uncovered shoulders, accompanied with more or less of the motion of washing with the same. This best agrees with much of the language of the Reformed Confessions which I have already cited, which again and again refer to the water as being poured, so as to rest on the body and to appear on it, and to make it clean and refresh it.

I now submit that, by the foregoing citations, I have reasonably established the following points, viz.:

a. That, whatever may have been the mode of baptism at the first organization of the Christian Church, sprinkling or affusion was used for the baptism of the sick within about one hundred years of the death of the apostle John; that it was sometimes employed in the fifth century for the baptism of the

---

[103] Quick, *Synodicon*, etc. ii: 447. "The Form and Manner of Baptizing Pagans, Jews, Mahometans, and Anabaptists converted to the Christian Faith," etc.

[104] The idea of course is, that the spread of Anabaptistic principles tended to diminish Infant baptisms, and so left the unbaptized to grow to adult years.

[105] I cite the original MS. now in keeping in the library of Parliament.

[106] *E. g.* The font still preserved at Austerfield, in or from which, 19-29 March, 1589-90, William Bradford, afterwards the second Governor of Plymouth Colony, was baptized, is dug out of a block of brown stone, the circular excavation being about 23 in. across, and 9 in. in depth at the central deepest point. It had descended to the base use of a water-trough for fowls, when rescued by American interest.

well; and that by the twelfth, a Council gave formal sanction to the equal validity of sprinkling, pouring and dipping.

b. That, although the rubric of the English Church from its beginning to this day has required the immersion of infants except in cases of physical disability, in point of fact the exception became the law before the time of our fathers; so that in the later portion of Elizabeth's reign, and through that of James I., as the rule, children were baptized by affusion.

c. That, following the lead of Calvin, the Reformed Churches made sprinkling, or affusion, the law of their creeds.

d. That the Anabaptists themselves at first administered their adult baptism by pouring.

e. That the Mennonites always did, and do, the same.

f.. That at the time of Mr. Smyth's change of view as to the validity of infant baptism — and, indeed, for more than ten years afterward — there is no evidence of the existence in Holland of *any* sect administering the rite in any other way than by pouring.

g. That this pouring was accompanied by rubbing, so as to represent the act of washing the body, or some part of it, clean from soil or stain, as a symbol of that washing of regeneration by which the Holy Spirit cleanses the redeemed soul.

In view of all which, I am prepared to conclude it as every way most probable, that when Mr. Smyth renounced the baptism of his youth, and took upon him that rite in a new form, he did so by affusion. To my mind this theory best explains his own language and that of others with regard to the transaction.

Thus he himself, in the book which he at once proceeded to publish to justify the step he had taken, habitually speaks of baptism as "*washing* with water;"[107] "the forme [of baptism] is *washing one into* the covenant;"[108] "the true forme of baptifm confifteth in three things: (1) *washing* with water; (2) a new creature; (3) into the name of Chrift, or into the Trinity;"[109] "therefor neceffarily we muft for having true baptifme repeat *washing in to* the name of the Father, Sonne & Holy Ghost."[110] So he asks: "how then can any man without great folly *wash with water* (which is the leaft & laft of baptifme) one [*i. e.* an infant] that is not baptized with the Spirit & cannot confeffe with the mouth; or how is it baptifme if one be *fo washed?*"[111]

In like manner Richard Clyfton, in his reply to the book which I have just been quoting, uses the same term in the like sense, *e. g.*: "it is fuch *a washing*

---

[107] *The Character of the Beaft*, etc. v.
[108] *Ibid.* 50.
[109] *Ibid.* 55.
[110] *Ibid.* 57.
[111] *Ibid.* v.

as preacheth unto vs the purging of our finnes by Chrift;"[112] "without this *wafhing with water* into the name of the Father, etc. it cannot be baptifme."[113] So he calls Smyth's new church "a *new wafhed* companie."[114] And he elsewhere makes it clear that by this term "washing" neither of them intended immersion, for, assuming that there is no difference between them as to that, he incidentally shows that he means sprinkling by it : " Concerning the forme of baptifm I confeffe it is the *fprinkling* of a fit fubject with water into the name of the Father, etc."[115]

Ainsworth also published in reply to Smyth, and in his reference to the new baptism he says :[116]

Mr. Smyth anabaptized himfelf with water, but a child could have done the like unto himfelf, who cannot perform any part of fpiritual worfhip : therefore *Mr. Sm.* anabaptizing himfelf with water did no part of fpiritual worfhip ; and confequently it was carnal worfhip, and fervice of the Divil. If he anfwer, that a child, though he could *caft water on himfelf*, & utter fuch words as he heard *Mr. Sm.* fpeak withal ; yet could he not preach or open the covenant as *Mr. Sm.* did, etc.

Lastly, it is of great interest in itself, while it may possibly throw a suggestion also upon a question of baptism which has been mooted on our side of the sea, that, in 1645, Roger Williams in his *Chriftenings make not Chriftians* — a little book for a long time lost, and only within the present year recovered, and reprinted from the probably unique copy in the British Museum — says the evangelization of the heathen must be brought about :[117]

By such Meffengers as can prove their lawfull fending and Commiffion from the Lord Jefus, to make Difciples out of all nations : and fo to baptize *or wafh them εις τὸ ὀνομα* into the *name* or *profeffion of the holy Trinity*, etc.

So, on another page of the same tract,[118] he says, had he been so minded, he could have brought the whole Indian "Countrey to have obferved one day in feven ; I adde to have received a *Baptifme* (or wafhing), etc."

I need only add under this branch of the subject one single further decisive testimony to the point, that, whatever the form of baptism resorted to on this occasion may have been, it was *not immersion*. I find it in a letter written at Amsterdam a few months after by Lubbert Gerrits to the Mennonite church at Leuwarden, in which, referring to Smyth and his company, he says :[119]

---

[112] *The Plea for Infants and Elder People concerning their Baptifme*, etc. (1610), 171.
[113] *Ibid.* 173.
[114] *Ibid.* vi.
[115] *Ibid.* 159.
[116] *A Defence of the Holy Scriptures, Worfhip and Minifterie, in the Chriftian Churches feparated from Antichrift*, etc. (1609), 69.

[117] *Chriftenings make not Chriftians, or A Briefe Difcourfe concerning that name Heathen, commonly given to the Indians. And also concerning that great point of their Converfion*, 16°, *pp.* ii. 22. [B. M. (E. 1189. [8.])] p. 17.
[118] *Ibid.* p. 11.
[119] Translated by Mr. Muller, and printed in *Evans*, i: 212.

Therefore, first of all, we ministers have, according to the desire of our brethren, summoned these English before us, and again most perfectly examined them as regards the doctrine of salvation and the government of the Church, and also inquired for the foundation *and form* of their *baptism*, and *we have not found that there was any difference at all, neither in the one nor the other thing, between them and us*, etc.

This verdict, within a twelvemonth, of a jury on the ground, cautious yet disposed to be friendly, must be conclusive as to the point that, after some fashion, the baptism of Smyth and his company was by pouring, and neither by sprinkling, strictly so called, nor dipping.

3. *Did Mr. Smyth first affuse himself, and then in like manner administer the ordinance to his associates?*

We shall best understand what was done, if we can first fairly put ourselves into sympathy with the state of mind out of which action grew. And we shall find that the single special advance which Mr. Smyth had made in the brief interval of time between his leading his people into non-fellowship with the "ancient" church, — the reasons of which were set forth, as we have seen, in his book of *Diferences*, etc. — and his inspiring them to dissolve and annul their previous organization, and covenant together upon a new basis, — the grounds of which were explained and urged in his book called *The Character of the Beaſt*, etc. — consisted in his seeming to himself to have discovered that the baptism which they all had received in childhood, and been satisfied with in their adult years down to that hour, was inadequate and unscriptural to that degree that with a good conscience it could no longer be tolerated as the fundamental basis of their Christian organization. It was suddenly revealed to him that that rite had been fatally defective in two respects.

In the first place, it had descended to them from the old time through a false church. They had separated themselves from the Church of England because of its unscriptural qualities, and yet they had not separated themselves from the baptism of that Church; which, in the last analysis, was none other than the very baptism of that Rome which they regarded as the mother of harlots and the fountain of spiritual abominations — as the Antichrist of the Word of God. As Antichrist, Rome had utterly corrupted and destroyed all the ordinances of Christ. So far as she was concerned, therefore, true baptism had ceased from among men. And since the Church of England had taken her baptism from Rome, that must also be null and void. So that Smyth insisted that all the Separatists: [120]

---

[120] *The Character of the Beaſt*, etc. p. iv. The Separatists who did not follow Smyth took the ground that the lapsed character of the Church of Rome could not vitiate its baptism. Thus Francis Johnson replied to him on this point (in Clyfton's *Advertiſement*, etc. p. 30] thus:

must either goe back to England, or go forward to *true* baptifme; & al that fhal in time to come feparate from England muft feparate from the baptifme of England, & if they wil not feparate from the baptifme of England their is no reason why they fhould feparate from England as from a falfe Church.

And in the second place, since infants cannot "confeffe with the mouth," to "wafh an infant into the Trinity is not true Baptifme;" true Baptism being "to be adminiftered vppon perfons confeffing their faith and their fins."[121] Whence to him it followed that he and all his company, having received the ordinance in their infancy, were still without it. Hence their ecclesiastical estate was fatally inadequate, and they were:[122]

a falfe Church falfely conftituted in the baptifm of infants, & their owne vnbaptifed eftate, . . . and their feparation, the youngeft & the fayreft daughter of Rome, is an harlot: For as is the mother fo is the daughter.

But if true baptism had ceased from among men, it was useless to journey hither and thither in any vain hope to find it. The only way in which the ordinance in its purity could be had, must be to originate it *de novo* — if scripturally that might be done. Smyth was of opinion that it could be. And after he had — as he thought — done it, he explained his views on the subject, as follows:[123]

Whereas you fay they [we] have no warrant to baptize themfelves, I fay, as much as you have to fet vp a true Church, yea fully as much: For if a true Church may bee erected which is the moft noble ordinance of the New Testament, then much more baptifme: & if a true Church can not bee erected without baptifme . . . you cannot deny . . . that baptifme may alfo bee recovered. If they muft recover them [the Church and baptism] men muft beginne fo to doe & then two men joyning together may make a Church . . . Why may they not baptize, feeing they cannot conjoyne into Chrift but by baptifme? . . . Now *for baptifing a mans felf ther is as good warrant, as for a man churching himfelfe:* For two men fingly are no Church, joyntly they are a Church, & they both of them put a Church vppon them felves, fo may two men put baptifme vppon themfelves: For as both thofe perfons vnchurched yet have powre to affume the Church each of them for himfelf with others in communion: fo each of them vnbaptized hath powre to affume baptifme for himfelf with others in communion: And as Abraham & John Baptift, & all the Profelites after Abrahams example, Exod. 12. 48. did adminifter the Sacrament vppon themfelves: fo may any man raifed vp after the Apoftacy of Antichrift, in the recovering of the Church by baptifme, adminifter it vppon himfelf in communion with others . . . And as in the Old Teftament every man that was vncleane wafhed himfelf: every Preift going to facrifice wafhed himfelfe in the Laver at the dore of the Tabernacle of the congregation: which was a type of baptifme, the dore of the Church, Tit. 2. 5. Every Mr. of a Family adminiftered the Paffover to himfelf & all of his Family: The Preift dayly Sacrificed

---

We hold that the Baptifme of Rome was as true Baptifme, as circumcifion in the Apoftafie of Ifrael vvas true circumcifion, and needed not to be renounced and repeated, etc.

[121] *The Character of the Beaft*, etc. p. iii.
[122] *Ibid.* p. vii.
[123] *Ibid.* pp. 58, 59.

for himself and others: A man cannot baptife others into the Church, himfelfe being out of the Church: Therefore it is Lawfull for a man to baptize himself together with others in communion, & this warrant is a plerophory for the practife of that which is done by vs.

The question may here arise why Mr. Smyth and his people in this emergency did not apply to the Mennonites in Amsterdam; who, having always repudiated infant baptism, and not being in succession from any Antichristian Church, might be supposed to be able to convey the ordinance in a form to them unobjectionable. I suggest four reasons. In the first place, the difference of language was clearly an obstacle to that full interchange of thought which might be desired before taking such a step.[124] In the second place, it is not impossible that Mr. Smyth and his people were not anxious, could it be fairly avoided, to invite any such unpopularity toward their new departure, as might have seemed inevitable were they to solicit the Dutch Anabaptism. In the third place, it is quite probable that at that time they felt themselves too much out of theological sympathy with the Mennonites, to be able in conscience to receive the most intimate rite of the Gospel from them;[125] and this the more that it was one of their chief arguments against infant baptism, that infants could not — indispensably — assent to "the true Fayth."[126] And in the fourth place, to have been baptized by the Mennonites may have involved joining their church, which they did not then wish to do — preferring to be a church by themselves.[127]

As, then, it seemed to be the only course open to them, and as Mr. Smyth, at the time, firmly believed that it was a course which they had undoubted Scriptural right to take, it was determined that the lost rite of a pure baptism — unalloyed by infant incapacity to receive it, on the one hand, or by Antichristian inability to convey it, on the other — should be once more originated on earth by them, and for them. The first step, naturally, was properly to clear the ground of all rubbish of the past. This was done by formal disavowal of the old baptism, and express dissolution and renunciation of their former church estate, including the abdication by its officers of all their func-

---

[124] When a few months later [12 Mar. 1609] a portion of Smyth's company were in correspondence with the Dutch, they added to their letter the following postscript (*Original MSS. Amsterdam*):

Wee have written in our owne tonge becaufe wee are not able to expreffe our mynds in anie other, and feeing you have an interpreter. And wee have bene much greeved fince our laft conference with you, becaufe wee difhonoured the truth of God much for want of fpeach, in that wee w're not able to utter that poore meafure of knowledg which God of his grace hathe given us.

[125] *The Character of the Beaft*, etc. in its *résumé* of opinion (pp. vii, viii) seems to make it clear that while Smyth and his followers had advanced somewhat toward the general Mennonite position in respect "to the Flesh of Christ," and the magistracy, they had not then adopted their distinctively Arminian views. Helwys, Murton and others, who subsequently cast Smyth out of the Church for these heresies, seem never fully to have adopted them.

[126] *Ibid.* 54.

[127] This seems an obvious suggestion, and I have met with it somewhere in the literature of the case, but, having mislaid the citation, I am now unable to recall the source.

tions and official character. They seem to have agreed together, and declared, that they were no longer members of Christ's Church; no longer baptized people; no longer pastor, deacons and flock; but simply individual believers desiring church fellowship and privilege according to a new manner which their more enlightened consciences could approve. That such a step was inevitable to their principles, lies on the face of them.[128] That it was actually taken, we have three credible witnesses. Richard Clyfton, who was resident in Amsterdam at the time, and whose calm and candid character, as evidenced in his books, is fully endorsed by Gov. Bradford,[129] says:[130]

> After this, *they diffolved their Church* (which before was conioyned in the fellowfhip of the Gofpel & profefsion of the true fayth) & *Mr. Smyth being Paftor thereof, gave over his office*, as did alfo *the Deacons*, and devifed to enter a new communion by renouncing their former baptifme, and taking upon them an other, etc.

John Robinson, long familiarly acquainted with all parties to the transaction, thus describes it:[131]

> Which was [*i. e.* the procefs of reorganizing the church, etc.] *as I have heard from themfelves*, on this manner: M. Smyth, M. Heluiffe, and the reft, *having utterly diffolved and difclaimed their former church ftate and miniftry*, came together to erect a new church by baptifm, etc.

And Richard Bernard, writing within a twelvemonth of what took place, says:[132]

> By this trick is he [Smyth] *difpaftored*, and is but among them as a private perfon, till he be again elected; this is moft true: And thus hath he beene off and on in the minifterie two or three times. He was made minifter by Bifhop Wickam: that by and by in Brownifme he renounced, & was made minifter by Trades men, and called himfelfe The Paftour of the Church at Gainsbrough: this hath he loft againe by his fe-baptifticke way till he be chofen againe.[133]

Standing thus together as a company of private persons seeming to them-

---

[128] *Ibid.* vii.
[129] *Dialogue.* Young, etc. 453.
[130] *Plea for Infants*, etc. v.
[131] *Of Religious Communion*, etc. Works (ed. 1851), iii: 168.
[132] *Plaine Euidences*, etc. 20.
[133] A closer acquaintance with this fact would have saved frequent inconclusive reasoning. Thus the Chicago *Standard* of 1 July, 1880, in an editorial to which I have already referred, said:

> In the company was another minister besides himself, Thomas Helwys, who had the same power to adminiſter the ordinance which Smyth had. Each could adminiſter the ordinance to the other, and no cutting of the knot would be called for. Indeed, in such circumstances, the resort to such a proceeding as the solemn baptizing of himself by Mr. Smyth, in order to qualify himself to baptize the rest, is so irrational and absurd as to seem out of the question in the case of persons such as John Smyth and Thomas Helwys are upon all hands admitted to have been

The following considerations impair the usefulness of the above remark, viz.: (1) Smyth had laid down his ministry for the second time, and had not yet been made a minister again; (2) Helwys up to this date had never been a minister; (3) if both had been and remained ministers, it would have been indeed an incredible absurdity for either of them — after having denounced their old baptism and church estate as fraudulent and false — to have proceeded in virtue of an official character solely dependent on that fraud and falsehood, to administer ministerial acts.

selves to have true faith and desiring baptism and church fellowship, it was natural that all should turn to him whose restless logic had created the exigency, for deliverance from it. John Robinson says he was told by some of them that: "there was fome ftraining of courtefy who fhould begin"[134]— probably because John Smyth, with all his forwardness, was essentially a truly modest and humble man,[135] who would be very likely at such a time to turn to Helwys or Murton[136] and urge one of them to act for all. But all looked with expectancy toward him. And so he went forward. What he did is to be determined by testimony — which does not appear to have begun to be conflicting until more than a century and a quarter had passed away.

I have shown elsewhere[137] that, at this time, these English immigrants seem to have mostly lived, and assembled, over on the southeast side of Amsterdam, in the neighborhood of the *Regulicrs-poort*. This was very near to the then city wall, and to the mouth of the *Amstel;* and I think of Smyth and his company as now meeting a short distance outside the fortifications on the bank of this river, or some little affluent, for the performance of their solemn service. I am the more persuaded of this from the fact that, as no prayer preceded the baptism,[138] it seems not improbable that the entire religious service, with the exception of the rite itself, took place subsequently in the room where they were accustomed ordinarily to worship. Thus gathered together, after quietly waiting until all with one consent had laid the duty of beginning upon himself, I conceive of Mr. Smyth — disrobed sufficiently to allow of the easy washing of the upper portion of his body by himself — as walking into the stream, lifting handfuls of water and pouring them liberally upon his own head, shoulders and chest, until clean and white they glistened under the purifying streams, solemnly repeating as he did so that formula which the Saviour bequeathed to his people to the end of time. Then, turning, I imagine him as receiving his associates, Helwys, Murton, Pygott, Seamer, Overton, Bromhead, Jessop, Hodgkins, Bywater, Grindal, Halton, and the others, not forgetting Mary Smyth, Ann Bromhead, Ursula Bywater, the Dickens sisters, and the rest, and, one by one, after the same manner, reinitiating each into the earthly

---

[134] *Works*, iii: 168.

[135] He who reads *The laft booke of Iohn Smith, called the retractation of his Errours, and the confirmation of the Truth* (the only known copy is in the library of the Minster, York, Eng.) will surely believe what I have said, as to this engaging element in the character of a many-sided man.

[136] That John Murton was in full sympathy with what was done is clear from his own words [*A Defcription of what God hath Predeftinated Concerning Man*, etc. (1620), 159]: "Some one muft Baptife, not being yet Paftor or Elder; For there muft be a Flocke, before a Shepherd, as were all the Churches of the Primitiue time, etc."

[137] *Congregationalism as Seen*, etc. 284.

[138] "Unto which [baptism] they alfo afcribed so great virtue, as that they would not fo much as pray together before they had it." John Robinson, *Works*, iii: 168.

kingdom of God. And I have ventured here to introduce, as possibly with considerable exactitude pictorially representing the service performed by Mr. Smyth upon himself, a tracing from an ancient engraving representing the self-baptism in earlier days of a "Hemerobaptist."

Turning, now, from fancy which may be truth, to fact which is sure to be truth, I present the following witnesses in evidence that, in this or some other manner, John Smyth, on this occasion, did baptize, first himself, and then his followers.

1. Mr. Smyth himself in his last tract, published after his decease, seems to avow and justify the act:[139]

Seeing ther was no church to whome we could Joyne with a Good confcience, to haue baptifme from them, *ther for wee might baptife our felues*: that this is fo the lord knoweth.

And again:[140]

Maister Hel. [wys] saith that although ther be churches alreadie eftablifhed, minifters ordained and facraments adminiftered orderly, yet men are not bound to Joyne to thofe former churches eftablifhed, but may being as yet unbaptifed baptife them felues (*as we did*) and proceed to build churches of them felves, etc.[141]

2. We have already in part cited Mr. Ainsworth as to the point of affusion. Let us return to note the full scope of his evidence. He says:[142]

Mr. Sm. anabaptized himfelf with water . . . Wherefore reading and preaching being joyned togither, as baptifing with water & preaching: he that condemns the one outward action becaufe a child can doe it, condemneth alfo the other by the like reafon. And *Mr. Sm.* having thus written of children, *and doon to himfelf*, etc. . . . *He anabaptized himself* and then *anabaptized others*, etc.

3. In like manner let us revert to John Robinson's full statement, viz.:[143]

As I have heard from themfelves . . . *Mr. Smyth baptized firft him felf, and next Mr. Helwiffe, and fo the reft*, making their particular confeffions. Now to let pafs . . . *his baptizing himfelf*, which was more than Chrift himfelf did, Matt. iii. 14: I demand into what church he entered by baptifm, etc.

4. Richard Clyfton (a present witness) devotes large space and long argument to the matter. I cull sentences here and there, only, sampling the squareness of the testimony which he gives as to the fact, viz.:[144]

---

[139] *The laft booke of Iohn Smith*, etc. 37.
[140] *Ibid.* 37.
[141] Compare with this the confession of Smyth and his sympathizers, when, in 1609, seeking admission to the Mennonite Church in Amsterdam:

"qui hunc errorem fuum agnofcunt, ejus que poenitentiae agunt, viz.: quod incoeperint fe ipfos baptizare, contra ordinem a Chrifto conftitutum, etc. [Autograph *MS. Mennonite Archives Amsterdam.* Evans [i: 209] gives this in an English translation.]

[142] *Defence*, etc. 69, 82.
[143] *Works*, iii: 168.
[144] *Plea for Infants*, etc. (1610), pp. 177–9, 180, 183, 185, 186, 224.

In my former answer I sayd that it can not be shewed that any man did ever baptife him felf without special commandement from God, etc. and you thus replie: "I fay, as much as you have to fet up a true Church," wherein you anfwere not directly to the point, but shift it of, with faying that you have as much power to fet vp baptifme, or baptife your selfe, as we to fet vp a Church: *for fuppofe we have not this power to fet vp a Church, then how is your action of baptifing your felfe iuftified?* . . . You muft bring like warrant from the Scripture, that *you being vnbaptifed, may baptife your felfe,* or els . . . your baptifme prove but a vayne fanfie . . . If *you that baptife your self* (being but an ordinary man) may this do, then may an other do the like, and fo every one baptife himfelfe . . . Confider you that are fo barren of proof *for the adminiftring of Baptifing to your felf,* that you can not shew one good reafon to warrant it to be lawful . . . And fo *Mr. Smyth was a Church, when he baptifed himfelf,* which is abfurd to think . . . Then I pray you, Sir, refolve me how you can *baptife your felf into the Church, being out of it,* yea, and where there was no Church? Or how could you baptife others, your felf being out of the Church? . . . Seing you have already chaunged your mind again *concerning your baptifing of your self* . . . In that you *baptifed your felfe, and others,* without lawful calling, etc.

5. In 1610 an able reasoner now known to us only by the initials of "I. H." prefixed to his book, published in London *A Defcription of the Chvrch of Chrift, etc., with fome Oppofitions and Anfwers of Defence . . . againft certaine Anabaptifticall and Erronious Opinions . . . maintained and practifed by one Maifter Iohn Smith . . . and a Companie of Englifh People with him now at Amfterdam in Holland, whome he hath there with himfelfe Re-baptifed.*[145] This writer says:

I pray you tell vs one thing Master *Smith?*

By what rule baptifed you your felfe? What worde or example had you for that in all the Scriptures? Doe you affirme the baptifme of children to be the marke of the Beaft, becaufe, you fay, there is no word nor example in all the Scripture, to proue that they may be baptifed: And yet durft you prefume without either word or example, *to baptife your felfe.* If you go about to proue that lawful which you haue done, by any word, or example in the Scripture, I fay you cannot fet one ftep forward to that purpofe, but you muft allow thereby the baptifme of Children. I maruell you did not preuent this obiection: which wil be as hard a bone for you to gnaw vpon, as you thinke the baptifme of Children is to vs. It was wonder you wold not receiue your baptifme firft, from fome one of the Elders of the Dutch Anabaptifts; but *you will be holyer then all, and fee how you haue marred all.*

6. In 1623 "Edmond Jeffop, who fometime walked in the faid errors with them," printed in London his *Difcovery of the Errors of the Englifh Anabaptifts,* etc. In this he thus speaks:[146]

Mr. *Smith* baptized himfelfe firft, and then Mr. *Helwis,* and *Iohn Morton,* with the reft.

If I fhould now demand of you your warrant, for a man to baptize himfelfe; I much maruell where you would finde fuch a practife in all the New Teftament of Chrift; I am fure it would be a tafke too hard for you to find.

---

[145] 4⁰. pp. viii, 120 [Bodleian. (Tanner. 196)] p. 23. | [146] 4⁰. pp. xii, 104. [Bodleian. (B. 4. 7. Linc.)] p. 65.

7. Lubbert Gerrits, a Mennonite minister, writing from Amsterdam to the Church at Leeuwarden early in 1610, referring to this case of Smyth, calls it [147] "the act of baptizing by which he *has baptized himself.*"

8. Another witness whom we have already seen to have a considerable familiarity with the subject, deserves special examination. It is Richard Bernard in his *Plaine Euidences: etc. directed againſt Mr. Ainſworth the Separatiſt, and Mr. Smyth the ſe-baptiſt, etc.* I cite a sentence here and there directly to the point before us: [148]

Notorious actes, wee may reade, haue made men remarkable, and haue gotten them names and titles for a memoriall of the facts and deeds done; why ſhould not hee [Smyth] then obtaine what worthily hee hath deſerued? hee is *Anabaptiſticall,* for rebaptization; and he is a *Se-baptiſt, becauſe hee did baptiſe himſelfe* . . . Mr. Smith did baptiſe, and was not before by his own judgment & profeſſion baptiſed; ſo a perſon vnbaptiſed did baptiſe: and therefore it is no true Sacrament by his owne doctrine . . . And therefore all his company haue receiued by him corruption . . . Hee hath (if you will beleeue him) recouered the true Baptiſme, and the true matter and forme of a true Church, which now is onely to be found pure among a company of *Se-baptiſts.* Mr. Smith will hold euer this word (Se) to himſelfe; for in going into Browniſme hee was a Separatiſt, he held differing opinions from them, and now that he is in Anabaptiſme hee is a Se-baptiſt . . . Baptiſme (ſaith he) is the doore into the Church: there muſte be then a Church, and a doore into the Church. I aſke therefore whether the viſible Church was among them or no, *when Mr. Smith did baptiſe himſelfe?* . . . As one falling to Anabaptiſme, leauing all Churches for that way, and *entering thereinto by baptiſeing of himſelfe,* whereby he is become Mr. Smith the Anabaptiſticall Se-baptiſt . . . [He holds] that true Baptiſme was nowhere to be had lawfully: *becauſe he did baptiſe himſelfe* . . . That in his caſe *he might baptiſe himſelf,* and ſo his Church be a pure Church, whence men may fetch true baptiſme, but lawfully belike no where elſe. Wofull premiſes, miſerable concluſion: errour and arrogancy void of true charitie . . . Mr. Smith *did baptiſe himſelfe* contrary to the Scripture (which commandeth one to baptiſe another, Mat. 28. 18.) and contrary to all examples in Scripture . . . It muſt needes then be a falſe baptiſing, with which all the reſt are polluted, etc.

9. So much for witnesses immediately cognizant of the facts. There are at least a dozen others, nearer and more remote in time, and circumstances, who might be marshalled to testify, but I will only here further refer to the careful judgment of a single writer — one who has the great advantage of being an antiquary, a Dutchman, and a Mennonite; who has spent his life in the Low Countries; who has the official custody of the manuscript remains of this very controversy; and who has for many years been a diligent and intelligent student of the history of the Separatists in Holland — I refer to Prof. J. G. de Hoop Scheffer, of the Mennonite College in Amsterdam. In a memoir lately read before the Royal Academy upon *The Brownists of Amsterdam,* and pub-

---

[147] See the whole letter, translated by Mr. Muller, in *Evans,* i: 211-213.

[148] 4°, pp. xvi, 340 [B. M. (4135. a.)], pp. 17, 18, 19, 20, 30, 314-315.

lished within the present year, upon the phase of the subject before us he says:[149]

In een plechtige godsdienstoefening, waarschijnlijk in October 1608, bediende hij eerst, na afgelegde belijdenis en ten aanschouwen van allen, den doop aan zichzelven, vervolgens aan Helwys en daarna aan de anderen, zoo velen 't begeerden en hun geloof beleden: ruim een veertigtal.	At a solemn religious service, probably in October, 1608, after making public confession, in the sight of all the others, *he* [Smyth] *performed the rite of baptism upon himself;* after which he baptized Helwys, and others who followed with confession of faith — to the number of about forty.

Here, now, we have first an antecedent probability growing out of the avowed opinions of the parties in interest, that a certain course would be adopted, and a certain act performed. We have next the direct declaration of the man immediately concerned, that that act did take place. We have then the corroborative statement of seven cotemporaries to the like effect. And we have, further, the express judgment, to the same end, of that modern scholar who by position, culture and opportunity has the best means to reach a candid and conclusive decision. All these unite to declare that John Smyth rebaptized first himself, and then his company.

And, what is remarkable, nobody *in those days* appears to have denied, or doubted, that he did thus. Again and again during Smyth's short life-time, and while Helwys and Murton still held their pens, was the act charged upon them, as an ecclesiastical irregularity needing justification, but that charge seems never to have been met by any attempt to deny its truth. One hundred and twenty-five years later good, but clumsy, Thomas Crosby — confessing that he had never seen Smyth's own books, which "are not to be met with" — suggested that those who charged him with Se-baptism:[150]

writ ... with so much paffion and refentment, that it is not unlikely fuch men might take up a report againft him upon flender evidence, and after one had publifhed it the others might take it from him without any enquiry into the truth of it, etc.

Seventy-three years later Joseph Ivimey improved upon Crosby's suggestion sufficiently with confidence to declare:[151]

There is no doubt but this silly charge was fabricated by his enemies, and it is an astonishing instance of credulity that writers of eminent talents have contributed to perpetuate the slander.

Seven years later still, Adam Taylor attributed it to misconstruction:[152]

---

[149] *De Brownisten Te Amsterdam gedurende den eersten Tijd na hunne Vestiging, in verband met het Ontstaan van de Broederschap der Baptisten,* etc. Amsterdam, 1881. 8°. pp. 176, p. 104.

[150] *History of English Baptists,* etc. (1738) i: 97.
[151] *History of English Baptists,* etc. (1811) i: 115.
[152] *History of English General Baptists,* etc. (1818) i: 85.

We may, therefore, presume, that the report of Mr. Smyth's baptizing himself originated in mistake: and has been perpetuated by those, who have too hastily taken up a report against their neighbour.

In our own time — since so many original data for judgment have been recovered — under the lead of Mr. Underhill a theory has been advanced that, inasmuch as, confessedly, the company originated among themselves a new baptism, it was for that reason that they were called *Se-baptists:* "not that each one dipped, or baptized *himself,* but [that] among them they commenced the practice."[153] So reasoning he reaches the result:[154]

I may, therefore, confidently affirm that the charge of baptizing himself is, with respect to Smith, a calumny, but arose from the circumstances referred to. In no other way can we account for the silence with respect to it, observed by himself in his writings, and [observed] in those of his friends.[155]

The Chicago *Standard* has gone so far as to intimate that writers in Holland at the time fell into this misapprehension:[156]

This language was construed by hostile writers as having the absurd meaning noticed above. *Something to the same effect Mr. Robinson heard, and honestly misconstruing it, reported it as what he had thus heard.* There is no other theory of the matter which in the light of candid history will stand the test.

The "times of ignorance" we have divine sanction to "overlook." But it is hard to entertain a doubt that, in view of the fuller and weightier evidence herein adduced, the candor of Baptist scholarship must henceforth concede: (1) that this was no more a case of immersion than of sprinkling, but of affusion; and (2) that John Smyth did affuse first himself, and then his company.

The remainder of this story may be brief. All testimony agrees that but very few months elapsed before Mr. Smyth moved on to another plane of thought and action; first suspecting and then affirming, that they had all been wrong in holding the right to baptize and — in his own phrase — to church, themselves; so that, really:[157]

their new-washed companie is no true church, and that there cannot be in a church the adminiſtratiō of baptifme & other ordinances of Chriſt, without Officers; contrarie to his former judgment, practife & writings.

Some modification of his theological views accompanied and exaggerated

---

[153] Dr. E. B. Underhill, in *Watchman,* 14 July, 1853.
[154] *Ibid.*
[155] Prof. S. S. Cutting [*Historical Vindications,* etc. (1859) 60] takes the same view.
[156] 1 July, 1880.
[157] Clyfton says [*Plea for Infants,* etc. vi] that this was the account given him at the time, by some of Smyth's church.

this difficulty, which soon constrained the majority of the new church, under the lead of Helwys and Murton, sorrowfully to excommunicate Smyth and twenty or thirty who thought with him. We have the statement made public by that majority as the justification of their course, as follows:[158]

> That it may not be thought we lay imputations, or caft reproaches upon Mr. Smyth unjuftly, we thought good, in fhort, to fet downe fome of the errors whereinto he is fallen, etc.:
>
> 1. That concerning CHRIST the firft matter of his flefh, he affirmed that all the Scriptures would not prove that he had it of the virgin Mary, but his fecond matter which he faid was his nourifhment, that the Scriptures proved he had of Mary, thus making CHRIST to have two matters of his flefh.
>
> 2. That men are juftified partly by the righteoufnefs of CHRIST apprehended by faith, partly by their own inherent righteoufnefs.
>
> 3. That Adams fin was not imputed unto any of his pofterity, & that all men are in the eftate of Adam in his innocencie before they commit actual fin; & therefore infants were not redeemed by CHRIST, but as the Angels & all other creatures.
>
> 4. That the Church & Minifterie muft come by fucceffion, contrary to his former profeffion in words & writings, & that by a fuppofed fucceffion he cannot fhew from whom, nor when, nor where.
>
> 5. That an Elder of one Church is an Elder of all Churches in the world.
>
> 6. That Magiftrates may not be members of CHRISTS Church, and retain their magiftracy.

Smyth and his friends, thus excluded, asked a church of the Mennonites to receive them, and a parley followed. It appears to have been objected against them that they had unwarrantably baptized themselves. Whereupon the following document, still preserved in the archives of that church in Amsterdam, was signed by sixteen men, and as many women, and offered to meet that difficulty:[159]

Nomina Ænglorum qui hunc errorem suum agnofcunt, ejufque pœnitentiae agunt, viz.: quod incœperint fe ipfos baptizare, contra ordinem a Chrifto conflitutum; quique jam cupiunt hinc veræ Chrifti ecclefiæ veniri, ea qua feri poffit expeditione. Cupimus unanimiter votum hoc noftrum ecclefiæ fignificari.[160]	The names of the Englifh people who confefs this their error, and repent of the fame, viz.: that they undertook to baptize themfelves contrary to the order laid down by Chrift; who now therefore defire to get back into the true Church of Chrift as fpeedily as may be. We are of one accord in the defire to have this our wifh fignified to the Church.

---

[158] *A Declaration of the Faith of Englifh People remaining at Amfterdam in Holland*, etc [Helwys's company] (1611) p. 16. This must be carefully diftinguifhed from another little book printed the year following with precifely the same title, with the exception of the addition: "being the remainder of Mr. Smyths Companie, etc." I have come to the knowledge of no copy of either except thofe preferved in the library of the Minfter at York, Eng.

[159] I have copied from the original MS. *Evans* [i: 244] has printed it.

[160] The names were thefe. A comparison of my list with that of Dr. Evans [i: 244] will show that I have read some of them differently from him.

Names of Men Hugo Bromhead, Gervase Nevill, John Smyth, Thomas Canadyne, Edward Hawkins, John Hardie, Thomas Pygott, Francis Pygott, Robert Staveley, Alexander Fleminge, Alexander Hodgkins,

Thereupon Helwys, Murton, William Pygott and Thomas Seamer, under date of 12 March, 1609, appealed to the Mennonite church thus addressed, begging them:[161]

> as you love the lord and his truth, that you will take wife councell, and that from Gods Word, how you deale in this caufe betwixt us and thofe that are juftlie for their finnes caft out from us.

After various considerations designed to persuade the church to be cautious in such an endorsement of the new applicants for their fellowship as should react against those who had felt constrained to cast them out, they conclude:

> Thus befeeching the lord to perfuade your hart, that your hand may not be againft his truth, and againft us the lords unworthie witneffes, wee take our leave, commending you to the gracious protection of the Almightie, etc.

The Mennonites appear to have been moved by this appeal, and took counsel of a sister church in the capital of Friesland. Considerable delay and several letters followed, all ending in the failure of the movement.[162]

Jan Munter was a friendly Waterlander. He owned a "Great Cake-House," or bakery, which appears to have had some sort of annex, where men might both meet and lodge. And in the hinder part of this John Smyth now seems to have taken refuge with his little band.[163] There was a curious resemblance between his spiritual history and that of Roger Williams, who went from a Congregational, through a Baptist Church, to be and remain a "Seeker" for the rest of his days; and Smyth, "inquiring after a new way of walking,"[164] and, to all appearance, unconnected with any church organization, spent here the brief remainder of his earthly life. For years a feeble man, in the summer of 1612 he fell sick with consumption.[165] And after seven weeks of increasing

---

John Grindal, Salomon Thomson, Samuel Halton, Thomas Dolphine, Mathew Pygott. (16.)
Names of Women. Ann Bromhead, Jane Southworth, Mary Smyth, Joane Halton, Allis Arnfield, Isabell Thomson, Margaret Staveley, Mary Grindal, Allis Pygott, Margaret Pygott, Betteris Dickens, Mary Dickens, Allis Paynter, Allis Parsons, Joane Briggs, Jane Organ. (16.)

[161] I have copied from the original MS. in the archives at Amsterdam. Dr. Evans [i: 209] has printed the letter, but—I suppose forgetting that new style had been adopted in Holland in 1583, and that the year (which still in England began 25 Mar.) there began 1 Jan.—has misstated the date as 12 Mar. 1610.

[162] Dr. Evans [i: 218] on the other hand represents the application as having been successful. But Prof. Scheffer in a letter before me intimates that Dr. E. has confounded this with a later request which was complied with:

This assertion of Dr. E. is quite hypothetical, and not at all probable; the records mention no other union with the English than the union [after Smyth had been dead some three years] of 1615.

[163] Prof. Muller, in *Evans,* i: 220.

[164] Clyfton, *Plea for Infants,* etc. vi. So in 1609, Ainsworth said [*Defence,* etc. 121] that God's hand "as it is heavie upon him already in giving him over from error to error ... fo wil the fame hand ftil follow him unto furder judgment if he do not repent."

[165] Bradford says [Young, *Dialogue,* etc. 451] "he [Smyth] died there [*i. e.* in Amsterdam] of a consumption, to which he was inclined before he came out of England."

debility,"¹⁶⁶ 1 September of that year he was borne from the Cake-House to his burial in the *Niewe Kerk*.¹⁶⁷

Late in 1614 what remained of his company renewed their old request for admission to one of the Mennonite churches, which, 20 Jan. 1615, was granted. For a short season a separate English service was held by them in the Cake-House, but it was not long before they became absorbed among the Dutch, leaving no trace of separate existence visible to history."¹⁶⁸

And so endeth the true story of John Smyth the Se-baptist, as told by himself and his contemporaries.

---

¹⁶⁶ His company said [*Declaration*, etc. 44]:

It pleased the lord at the legth, to vifit him with ficknes, and with a difeafe wherby he perceived that his life fhould not long continue; yet remayning about seaven weakes, during the which space, he behaved himfelf Chriftianlike.

¹⁶⁷ Burial Records, *Niewe Kerk*, sub dato.

¹⁶⁸ Prof. Muller, as cited by *Evans*, i: 220-223.

CHAPTER II.

AN INQUIRY WHETHER DIPPING WERE A NEW MODE OF BAPTISM IN ENGLAND IN, OR ABOUT, 1641.

IN the year 1876 Mr. Robert Barclay published in London the judgment that "the practice of immersion appears to have been introduced in England, on the 12th September, 1633."[1] Four years later I ventured to print a somewhat similar opinion, supported by such evidence as was then in my possession.[2] My statement was at once challenged by Baptist reviewers. One called it "an amazing error."[3] Another declared that "the unbroken tradition among Baptists is in favor of their immersion."[4] Another knew "of no reason to doubt that they [Baptists] all were immersed before the year 1641."[5] And still another insisted that "no fact in history is more certain than that they have *always* immersed."[6]

I did not know very much about the subject then. But I have since studied it as opportunity has offered; and I now propose to set down the results of that investigation.

It seems very safe to say that any change like that involved in making conscience of one particular form of the administration of a church rite over other forms, possible and actual; must — with human nature what it always has been — provoke difference of feeling, and the expression of it. And since the art of printing was discovered, it seems equally safe to decide that that kind of argumentation would leave its trace upon the literature of the time. Were anything of the sort to take place now, it would breed a tremendous discussion in the columns of the religious newspapers. Two centuries and a half ago — nearly or quite two hundred years before the founding of journals which could have been so employed — such a controversy must necessarily have been carried on through the medium of books, pamphlets and broadsides. We may lay it down then as certain, that, if at any time in the seventeenth century any

---

[1] *Inner Life of the Relig. Societies of the Commonwealth*, etc. 73. The date is the one given in the Kiffin *MS.* as that of the founding of Spilsbury's church in London. Ivimey, i: 139.
[2] *Congregationalism as Seen*, etc. 318.
[3] New York *Examiner and Chronicle*, 19 Aug. 1880.
[4] Prof. Heman Lincoln, D D., Newton Theo. Sem. in the Boston *Watchman*, 14 Oct. 1880.
[5] Portland *Zion's Advocate*, 28 July, 1880.
[6] Chicago *Standard*, 1 July, 1880.

question arose among good people in England as to the necessity of the substitution of immersion for affusion or sprinkling, as the sole mode of baptism; books, pamphlets and broadsides were printed about it — for and against — which, if still in existence and to be found, would give us in the most authentic manner ample and accurate knowledge as to what was done, and why it was done. Such literature, however, is proverbially ephemeral, and except as it may have been preserved in some extraordinary way, and for some special end, it would hardly be reasonable to anticipate, at this late date, any large success in its recovery.

But it so happens that at the exact time when this question of immersion — if there were any such question — must have arisen, Providence raised up a man whom it inspired with the idea of gathering together, and dedicating to the uses of the future, *every issue of the press, of whatsoever sort it might be.* This was the royalist bookseller, George Thomason, of the Rose and Crown, in St. Paul's Churchyard. It appears to have been in 1641 that the idea first forcibly struck him that there would be both interest and value in thus collecting and preserving the multifarious publications which the ferment of those new times in Church and State was breeding thick and fast. He seems to have begun, retrospectively, by procuring all on which he could lay his hand which had seen the light during the few previous months. And then for twenty years — and what years they were! — down to 1662, he made it his business to let nothing licensed, surreptitious, or secret escape him. He even copied with his own hand "near one hundred feveral [manuscript] pieces, moft of which," he says, "were on the kings fide, which no man durft venture to publifh here without the danger of his ruin." This wonderful collection he arranged chronologically — taking "exact care" that "the very day is written upon [the title-page of] moft of them that they came out" — and bound in 2220 volumes — folio, quarto, and smaller, according to the size of their contents — aggregating, it is estimated, nearly 34,000 separate publications. It is a curious miscellany, and the chronological necessity of it makes strange bedfellows. An almanac lies sandwiched between a sermon and a squib; a treatise on turnips may crowd an epithalamium on one side and an elegy on the other; vulgar and nasty "Mercurius Philalethes" leans and leers between John Milton and Jeremy Taylor; and tracts on Church Government, engineering, agriculture, wine, wool and witchcraft, may be looked for in the close company of sailors' songs, catechisms, goodwives' gossip, round-head rhymes and loyalist lampoons.[1]

---

[1] The facts and citations in this description are taken from Thomason's preface to his MS. catalogue of his collection, etc. The best brief published account is perhaps that in E. Edwards's *Memoirs of Libraries: including a Handbook of Library Economy*, etc. (1859) i: 455.

It seems a curious thing that no English Baptist scholar appears to have thought it worth his while to examine consecutively this collection — now known as the "King's Pamphlets"[8] in the library of the British Museum — with reference to the question under discussion; and that it should have been left for an outsider, and an American, to undertake it. But during the last winter I devoted some days to that work, and was rewarded by the discovery of no fewer than *one hundred and eighty* separate publications bearing directly upon the Baptist controversy; — the majority of which were printed within the first ten years after the date alleged by Mr. Barclay as that of the origin of the practice of immersion in England. I kept a register of my findings, with their press marks, which — expanded to cover the remainder of that century — I add at the end of this tract, for the benefit of whomsoever it may concern; and, to save space, I shall herein cite such treatises included therein as I may have occasion to refer to, simply by their author's name, or the first word or two of the heading of such as are anonymous, with their number in that list, leaving the reader to get the entire title from the Appendix.

The earliest date at which immersion was publicly and officially announced as being held needful by English Baptists, was 16 Oct. 1644;[9] at which time appeared *The Confession of Faith of those Churches which are commonly (though falsly) called Anabaptists*, etc. which was "subscribed in the names of seven churches in London," by fifteen persons, the first of whom was William Kiffin. The XLth article is as follows, viz.:[10]

That the way and manner of the dispensing this ordinance, is dipping or plunging the body under water; it being a figne, must answer the things signified, which is, that intereft the Saints have in the death, burial, and resurrection of Chrift: And that as certainly as the body is buried under water, and risen again, so certainly shall the bodies of the Saints bee raised by the power of Chrift, in the day of the resurrection, to reigne with Chrift. [There is an appended note: The word *Baptizo* signifies to dip or plunge, (yet fo as convenient garments be both upon the Administrator and subject, with all modefty.)]

The practical question now to be considered is whether this requirement of dipping had been accepted from the rise of distinctively Baptist sentiments in England, or whether plunging had been superinduced upon another and different earlier practice; and, if so, at what date. And, waiving the inquiry whether there had been, at some time previous to 1600, Baptist churches in that country which had lost visibility, the question respects such Baptist churches there as survived, or had grown up between that year and the period

---

[8] They get this name because George III., in 1762, spent £300 in making a present of the collection, after various fortunes and perils, to the British Museum.

[9] This is the date of publication endorsed on its face by Thomason.
[10] App. 35, p. 20.

of the publication of the Confession just cited — that is, in the first four and forty years of the seventeenth century.

It seems to be conceded on all hands that when Helwys and Murton recrossed the German Ocean from Holland, in or about 1612,[11] the church which they founded in Newgate was the first Baptist church, and the only one then in England in that century. By 1626 we can trace possibly ten others, making eleven in all, viz.: those in London, Lincoln, Tiverton, Salisbury, Coventry,[12] Stoney Stratford,[13] Ashford, Biddenden and Eyethorn in Kent,[14] Canterbury,[15] and Amersham in Buckinghamshire.[16]

These were all General Baptist churches; that is to say, they more or less leaned toward Arminianism in their theology; but Crosby took pains to declare[17] "that this difference in opinion is not a sufficient or reasonable ground of renouncing Chriſtian communion with one another," and so makes no distinction between them and the Particular, or Calvinistic, Baptists in his history.[18] It seems to be further safe to conclude — from their own language;[19] from the practice of the Dutch Mennonites with whom they were in fellowship;[20] from the concession of the latest and most learned English Baptist historian;[21] and from evidence yet to be presented in another form — that these Baptist churches did not practice immersion. Besides these, there appear to have been many other opponents of infant baptism, who were not as yet affiliated on that basis, but were scattered about in various Puritan churches, indistinguishably from their other members. Thus Crosby says[22] that, down to 1633, the Baptists had been "intermixed among other Proteſtant Diſſenters,

---

[11] It used to be said that this was in 1614 [*Taylor*, i: 87; Price, *Hist. Mod. Noncon.* etc. i: 519], but *Evans* [i: 224], and *Skeats* [41] put it in 1612. Perhaps this latter date finds confirmation in the fact that the Bodleian contains a presentation copy of Helwys's *Short Declaration* to the king, with an autograph note [from Helwys] on the fly-leaf, which is signed "Spittlefield near London." Assuming that such a copy would be sent early, if at all, the date of the book, which is 1612, would seem to make Helwys resident near London at that date.

[12] The first five are named in a letter of C. C. Aresto, 3 Nov. 1626, in *Evans*, ii: 24, 26.

[13] *Evans*, ii: 54.

[14] *Ibid.* ii: 56; *Taylor*, i: 283, 281.

[15] *Ivimey*, i: 138; *Taylor*, i: 162.

[16] *Taylor*, i: 96.

[17] *Crosby*, i: 173.

[18] Ivimey also [i: 137] claims that General Baptist Church at Canterbury referred to above, as a regular Baptist Church.

[19] Helwys uniformly calls baptism *waſhing*, not dipping: *e. g.* [*Short Declaration*, etc. p. 168] "You wil have infants baptized, that is *waſhed with water* and certen words;" [p. 139] "he that denies *waſhing*, or is not *waſhed* with the spirit is not baptized, and hee that denies *waſhing*, or *is not waſhed with water* is not baptized; becauſe we ſee the Baptiſme of Chriſt is to bee *waſhed* with water and the Holie Ghost."

[20] There remain in the archives of the Mennonite Church in Amsterdam six letters, of date from 3 Jan. 1624 to 5 June 1631, manifesting fellowship and asking advice, which passed between these English churches and the Mennonites. Prof. Muller translated the letters, and Evans [ii: 21-51] printed the translations.

[21] Evans [ii: 52] says:

In this opinion [viz.: that these churches were not immersionist] Dr. Muller fully agrees. But was it so? We cannot pronounce positively, but are bound to confess that the probabilities are greatly in its favor. The harmony of opinion, and the anxiety for agreement, which their Dutch brethren manifested in the documents laid before our readers [the six letters aforesaid], would *more than warrant this concluſion*.

[22] i: 147.

without diftinction, and so confequently fhared with the Puritans in all the perfecutions of thofe times," and later historians [23] mainly endorse his view. It is obvious that all such Baptists, while free to withhold their children from baptism, must themselves have been baptized in the same manner as had all others around them, and could not as yet have made the necessity of dipping an article of their faith. This brings us down to within eleven years of the issuance of the first distinctively Immersionist Confession of Faith, above cited, when we strike the formation of Mr. Spilsbury's Baptist Church in Wapping, by amicable separation from the first Independent Church of Henry Jacob and John Lathrop, the date assigned to which is 12 Sept. 1633. It has been usual — I think I may say nearly universal — to claim that this church was founded on the issue of immersion, and began with that form of baptism. Crosby says he derived his information from "an antient manufcript, *faid* to be written by Mr. William Kiffin, who lived in thofe times, and was a leader among thofe of that perfuafion." [24] Conceding the genuineness of this manuscript, and its value in testimony — both of which might be open to question — let us note its exact words as to the point before us: [25]

There was a congregation of Proteftant Diffenters of the independant Perfuafion in London, gather'd in the year 1616, whereof Mr. Henry Jacob was the firft paftor; and after him fucceeded Mr. John Lathorp, who was their minifter at this time. In this fociety feveral perfons, finding that the congregation kept not to their firft principles of feparation, and being alfo convinced that *baptifm was not to be adminiftred to infants, but fuch only as profeffed faith in Chrift*, defired that they might be difmiffed from that communion, and allowed to form a diftinct congregation, in fuch order as was moft agreeable to their own fentiments.

The church, confidering that they were now grown very numerous, and fo more than could in thefe times of perfecution conveniently meet together, and believing alfo that thofe perfons acted from a principle of confcience, and not obftinacy, agreed to allow them the liberty they defired, and that they fhould be conftituted a diftinct church; which was perform'd the 12th of Sept. 1633. And as they believed that *baptifm was not rightly adminiftred to infants, so they look'd upon the baptifm they had receiv'd in that age* [*i. e.* in infancy] *as invalid:* whereupon moft or all of them received a new baptifm. Their minifter was Mr. John Spilfbury. What number they were is uncertain, becaufe in the mentioning of the names of about twenty men and women, it is added, "with divers others."

In the year 1638, Mr. William Kiffin, Mr. Thomas Wilfon, and others, being of the fame judgment, were upon their requeft, difmiffed to the faid Mr. Spilfbury's congregation.

In the year 1639, another congregation of Baptifts was formed, whofe place of meeting was in Crutched-Fryars; the chief promoters of which were Mr. Green, Mr. Paul Hobfon and Captain Spencer.

It has been common to represent that Mr. Spilsbury at this time went over

---

[23] *Taylor,* i: 97; *Evans,* ii: 51.   [24] i: 100.   [25] *Ibid.* i: 148.

to Holland to obtain immersion; which of course would settle it that such was the method adopted by this church. But that statement seems to have had its origin as late as 1669 from Wall, who, in his *Plain Discovery*, etc.[26] mentions it as a rumor which he had heard some years before in London that Spilsbury visited Holland to be baptized of Smyth. He did not know that poor Smyth, in 1633, had been dead more than twenty-one years, nor that he never baptized by immersion. And Hercules Collins (1691) stigmatizes the whole story as "absolutely untrue," which Crosby reaffirms.[27]

Moreover, we find Mr. Spilsbury himself earnestly and forcibly arguing that, under certain circumstances, unbaptized persons have the right to originate baptism — summing up with this conclusion,[28] viz.:

> By all which it appears that baptizedneffe is not effential to an Adminiftrator, and therfore we ought not to ftay without when Chrift the Porter opens, and invites us in.

All of which would be very unnatural if Wall's story were true of him.

So that we are remitted to the language of Kiffin's account uncolored from without, for our knowledge of what was done. Examining it carefully, we discover four things, viz.: (1) that the seceders from Lathrop's church had given up infant baptism; (2) that having been themselves baptized in infancy, and being convinced that the valid ordinance required the profession of faith in Christ on the part of the recipient, they wished to be again baptized; (3) that "most, or all of them" did, therefore, receive "a new baptism;" but (4) there is neither statement, nor hint, that this new baptism was by immersion. I have found no such hint in the autobiography — edited by Orme in 1823[29] — of Kiffin, who curiously says nothing whatever, in his account of himself, of his becoming a Baptist; nor in his memoir published by Ivimey in 1833.[30] There is nothing, then, to interfere with the supposition that the "new baptism" received by this church was by affusion; leaving them in precisely the same situation with the eleven churches already traced, which had preceded them. I do not now affirm that this was the fact; but I do insist that there is nothing in the statements describing the origin of this church of Mr. Spils-

---

[26] No. 274, p. 45.

[27] Collins [*Believers Baptism*, etc. No. 358, p. 115] says:

Could not the Ordinance of Chrift which was loft in the Apoftafy be rev.ved . . . unlefs in fuch a filthy way as you faffly affert, viz : that the Englifh Baptifts received their Baptifm from Mr. John Smyth? *It is absolutely untrue*, it being well known by fome yet alive how falfe this Affertion is.

And *Crofby* [i: 103] says " Mr. Spilfbury was *fulfly reported* to have gone over to Holland to receive baptifm from John Smyth," etc.

[28] *Gods Ordinance, the Saints Priviledge*, etc. [No. 81] p. 10.

[29] *Remarkable Paffages in the life of W. Kiffin, written by himself, and edited from the original MSS. with notes, by W. Orme* (1823), etc. 8°. pp. xxiv, 162. [B. M. (1124. e. 2.)]

[30] *The Life of Mr. W. Kiffin, upwards of sixty years* [1639-1701] *Pastor of the Baptist Church Devonshire Square London*, etc. 8°. pp. xiv, 110. [B. M (1126. i. 13.)]

bury inconsistent with such a theory, provided evidence from any other quarter shall be seen to favor it.

The same remark is true of the church in Crutched-Friars formed in 1639. So that we come down to a period within about four years of the date of the first English Anabaptist Confession, without finding any *proof* of the existence of immersion in England. We have testimony which would bear interpretation in its favor, were that made necessary by other considerations; but which is equally compliant with a different theory, should that be established.

Let us now examine the quality of the suggestions made by the literature of that day, as to the question before us.

I begin with *Anabaptisme's Mysterie*, etc.[31] (1623) which contains a letter from an Anabaptist, giving his reasons for leaving the Church of England. He says:

> The thing wherein I differ from the Church of England is, they fay at their *wafhing*, or baptizing, in their Infancy, They are mēbers, children of God, and inheritours of the kingdom of heaven. This I dare not beleeve; for the fcriptures of God declare that neither flefh nor *wafhing* the flefh can fave ... The confequence of this is, that Infants are not to bee baptized, nor can bee Chriftians; but fuch onely as confeffe their Faith, as thefe fcriptures teach.

Not one word is said by the Anabaptist of any question about the *mode* of baptism — nor is there an allusion to that department of the subject in I. P[reston]'s five and fifty pages of comment on this letter. Whence I infer that, at that date, the mode had not become a subject of discussion in England.

In 1641 R. Greville — better known as Robert, Lord Brooke — published a *Discovrse*[32] in which having occasion to refer to the Anabaptists of that time in England, he said, they:

> only deny Baptifme to their Children till they come to yeares of difcretion, and then they baptize them; but *in other things they agree with the Church of England.*

Nearly at the same time, the author of *A Difcovery of 29. Sects*, etc.[33] thus describes the Anabaptists, viz.:

> Thefe men fet themfelues wholly againft the Doctrine of John the Baptift, except onely in this that they will baptize with Water, *but they will not doe it whileft they are children, till they be able to anfwer for themfelues.* They write themfelues Members and Children of God, and certaine inheritours of the Kingdome of Heauen.

These testimonies I think imply that down to the time when they were written — which would be the last of 1640, or the early months of 1641 —

---

[31] No. 2, p. 2. Crosby's reprint of this letter [i: 134] is not minutely accutate.
[32] *A Difcovrfe opening the Nature of that Epifco-pacie, which is exercifed in England*, etc. 4°. pp. viii, 124. [B. M. (E. 177. [22.])] p. 96.
[33] No. 4, p. 5.

public attention had not yet been called to dipping as being insisted upon by the Baptists as a fundamental article of their creed.[34]

We have, in the same year (1641), the first evidence which I have discovered that the subject of baptism, as connected with any novel mode of administration, was attracting the notice of observers; although its bearings are by no means clear. It occurs as an appendix to a very brief Vindication of the Book of Common Prayer, being entitled *A Difcovery of a fort of people called Re-baptifts, lately found out in Hackney Marfh, neere London*, etc.:[35]

About a Fortnight fince a great multitude of people were met going towards the River in Hackney Marfh, and were followed to the water fide, where they all were Baptized againe, themfelues doing it one to another; fome of which perfons were fo feeble and aged, that they were fayne to Ride on Horfe-backe thither. This was wel obserued by many of the Inhabitants living there abouts, and afterwards one of them Chriftened his owne Child, and another tooke upon him to Church his owne wife, an Abominable Act, and full of groffe Impiety.

There is nothing here to imply immersion more than affusion as the mode, nor is it easy to explain the latter two averments into consistency with anything likely to be done by the Baptists; so that I am inclined to dissociate the whole transaction from them, and look upon it as merely an incidental illustration of that unsettledness, and disposition toward novelties, which were about that time [36] beginning powerfully to affect the English mind.

We now reach the first of several very decided testimonies. In April, 1642,[37] one "P. B." published a *Discourse* favoring the Baptism of children. This was the well-known Praise-God Barbon,[38] whom both Ivimey [39] and Brook [40] represent to have been a Baptist and the pastor of a Baptist church, and who really was closely connected with them; but whose two books which have been preserved, show him, while on friendly terms with the Baptists — "fome of which are my loving friends and acquaintance, whom I would not difpleafe, but rather pleafe; whom I envy not, but love; but the truth is to be loved above

---

[34] Richard Baxter [*Reliquiæ Baxterianæ*, etc. 41] says, under a date which seems to be either 1641 or 1642, that at Gloucester he met with the first Anabaptists he had ever seen: "about a dozen young Men, or more, of confiderable Parts, had received the Opinion againft Infant Baptifm, and were rebaptized, and laboured to draw others after them." But he says nothing about their insisting on any particular mode of administration.

[35] No 5. p. 8.

[36] The famous "Root and Branch" petition, praying that the government of Bishops with all its Dependencies, Roots and Branches, be abolished, had been sent to Parliament the previous December.

[37] "April, 1642," is Thomason's endorsement across the title-page.

[38] Misled by the endorsement, in what seemed to be a contemporary hand-writing, across the title-page of a copy in my possession, in the Bibliographical Collections in the Appendix of *Congregationalism as Seen*, etc., I wrongly attributed this [No. 883] to "P. Bakewell." But Thomason's endorsement refers it to Barbon, while Kilcop [*Short Treatife*, etc. No. 7, p. 8] in replying to the book says: "thus did Praisgod Barbon of late;" citing passages showing beyond mistake his reference to this tract.

[39] i: 157.

[40] iii: 399.

all, being moſt deare and precious"[41] — to have radically opposed their views on the subject in hand. He says:[42]

> The way of *new* Baptizing, *lately* began to be practiſed by ſome ſuppoſing themſelves, and ſo others, not to have bin Baptized with the Baptiſme of Christ, hath no ground, etc. . . .
> But now *very lately* ſome are mightily taken, as having found out a new defect in the Baptiſme under the defection, which maketh ſuch a nullitie of Baptiſme, in their conceit, that it is none at all; and it is concerning *the manner of Baptizing*, wherein they have eſpyed ſuch default as it maketh an abſolute nullity of all perſons Baptiſme but ſuch as have bin *ſo Baptized according to their new diſcovery*; and ſo partly as before in regard of the ſubject, and partly in regard of ſo great default in the manner: They not only conclude, as is before ſayd, a nullity of their preſent Baptiſme, And ſo but addreſſe themſelves *to be Baptized a third time after the true way and manner they have found out*, which they account a precious truth. *The particular of their opinion and practiſe is to Dip, and that perſons are to be Dipped, all and every part to be under the Water*; for if all the whole perſon be not under the Water, then they hold they are not Baptized with the Baptiſme of Chriſt. As for Sprinkling, or pouring Water on the Face, it is nothing at all as they account, and ſo meaſuring themſelves by theſe *new* thoughts, as unbaptized, they addreſſe themſelves to take it up after the manner of Dipping. . . . Baptiſme [they reaſon] is a Buriall, as it is written, We are Buried with him in Baptiſme, &c., and we are raiſed up alſo to newneſſe of life. This Buriall and reſurrection, only Dipping can import and hold forth. Whereunto I ſay it is very true, that Baptiſme is a Buriall, and holdeth forth our Buriall and riſing with Chriſt. And ſo it is [alſo] in regard of the perſon that is Baptized by Sprinckling, or powring Water on the Face, as they are pleaſed to ſay, they are under the water, and Buried. I deſire they would ſhew how elſe they were Baptized unto Moſes in the Cloud and in the Sea, when not ſo much as an hair of their heads was wet . . .
> And furthermore to reſolve and determine how this totall dipping can ſtand with modeſty and ſhamfaſteneſſe, is a hard matter to be made apparant. If out of modeſty perſons ſhall uſe a linnen garment, or the like, it will be very conſiderable [*i.e.* it will require to be carefully conſidered], whether this is not to be modeſt above what is written, etc. . . .
> I hope when they have *further conſidered* this matter, they may abate of the fierceneſs of their opinion: ſo as to thinke that Baptiſme under the defection may be Gods ordinance, *ſo as there ſhall be no need of this new dipping.*
> But inaſmuch as this is *a very new way*, and the full growth of it, and ſettling *is not yet known, if it be to themſelves, yet not to me and others:* I will forbeare to ſay further to it.

Careful reading will find three things here declared, viz.: (1) that certain Baptists were then insisting on dipping as essential to true Baptism; (2) that this view — in the spring of 1642 — had been very recently for the first time advocated and acted upon; and (3) that its adoption by some had led them to submit to the rite for the third time [43] — which last renders necessary the con-

---

[41] *Diſcourſe*, etc. [No. 6] p. iv.
[42] *Ibid.* pp. 3, 12, 13, 15.
[43] Barbon refers to this in another place [p. 11]: "here is no ground to goe upon, but that which leadeth into an endleſſe Labyrinth: and, indeed, this ſome of them have come to ſee and to confeſſe, and ſo have rejected their ſecond Baptiſme alſo, and taken up a third, which in time no doubt, when their heate is over . . . they will ſee it to be as faulty as their first or ſecond, etc." N. Homes in his *Vindication*, etc. (1645) [No. 77, p. v] describes an actual case, as follows:

clusion that the English Baptists who had felt bound in conscience to be rebaptized as adults, had been hitherto sprinkled or affused; obliging them, when they afterwards took up the idea of dipping, to be baptized still again."

Four treatises on the other side followed Mr. Barbon's volume within three months; one by Thomas Kilcop [45] in May, one by Edward Barber in May,[46] and one in June by "A. R.,"[47] followed by a *Second Part*,[48] in July, from the same author. Kilcop refers to Barbon's book, and replies to one of his arguments. Barbon [49] had questioned the right of the Baptists, if they did think true baptism to have been lost from the earth, to restore the same without special warrant from heaven. Kilcop answers: [50]

Every Scripture that gives you warrant, or any of your judgement, to erect a Church ſtate, gives us the ſame warrant to erect baptiſme, ſith the one cannot be done without the other, for none can put on Chriſt (that is viſibly by outward profeſſion) but ſuch as are baptiſed into Chriſt, etc.

But he makes no allusion whatever to Barbon's charge of the newness of the dipping way.

Barber's treatise bears on its title-page the date of 1641. But the book contains internal evidence carrying it over at least to May, 1642, as its earliest possible date of issue.[51] He replies to Barbon in the same manner as Kilcop had done; [52] but makes no further reference to the charge of the newness of the dipping way, than is involved in saying in his preface: [53]

Beloved Reader, it may ſeeme ſtrange that in theſe times when ſuch abundance of Knowledge of the Goſpell is profeſſed in the World, there ſhould notwithſtanding be generally ſuch ignorance, eſpecially in and amongſt thoſe that profeſſe themſelves Miniſters thereof, of that glorious principle, True Baptiſme or Dipping . . . and that the Lord ſhould, amongſt ſome others, *raiſe up mee, a poore Tradeſman, to devlge* [divulge] *this glorious Truth* . . . The Lords uſuall dealing it being to bring mighty things to paſſe by weake meanes, as . . . where the walls of Jerecho fell down by the blaſts of Rams hornes, etc.

One congregation at firſt adding to their Infant-Baptiſme the adult baptiſme of ſprinkling; then not reſting therein, endeavouring to adde to that a dipping, even to the breaking to peeces of their congregation. Since that the Miniſter firſt dipped himſelfe. Not contented therewith, was after baptized by one that had onely his Infante Baptiſme.

[44] I beg to say here, once for all, that I fully appreciate the objection which our Baptist brethren logically make, from their premises, to the using of the term "baptized again," when one, sprinkled in childhood, is affused or immersed in after life. I use the term not with purpose of offense to them, but simply as true from *my* standpoint, and the most convenient way, without lengthened circumlocution, of stating the facts.

[45] No. 7.
[46] No. 8.
[47] No. 9.
[48] No. 10.
[49] *Diſcourſe*, etc. p. 6. [referring to the case of Nadab and Abihu, Lev. x.]
[50] *Short Treatiſe*, etc. [No. 7] p. 10.
[51] *E. g* [p. 27.] "Since part of this Treatiſe was in Preſſe, there came to my hand a Booke, ſet forth by P. B. (No. 6, published Apr. 1642) which could I have gotten ſooner, I ſhould have answered more fully, etc."
[52] *Small Treatiſe*, etc. [No. 8] p. 27.
[53] *Ibid.* p. ii.

"A. R." has in his Second Part the following plea in mitigation of this charge of newness, etc.:[54]

If any fhall thinke it ftrange and unlikely, that all the godlieft Divines and beft Churches fhould be thus deceiued in this point of Baptifme for fo many yeares together [*i.e.* as never before to know that true baptism is dipping, and dipping alone true baptism]: let them confider that all Chriftendome (except here and there one, or fome few, or no confiderable number) was fwallowed up in groffe Popery for many hundred yeares before Luthers time, which was not untill about 100. yeares agone.

We may note here, in passing, a similar plea advanced eleven years later by W. Kaye in his *Baptifme without Bafin*, etc. (1653), thus:[55]

Q. How comes it then to pafs that this Doctrine of Baptifme [dipping] *hath not been before revealed?*
A. [in part] In difcovery whereof, the Church *begins* to be reftored to the purity of the primitive time of Chrift and his Apoftles.

At some time during 1642 one "R. B." also replied to Mr. Barbon in a book[56] which has thus far eluded my search, but which led Barbon to write a reply, which came out 14 April, 1643. In the course thereof he utters himself as follows, viz.:[57]

New things are very pleafant, and many are much taken with them, as is R. B. with *dipping;* about which he taketh great paines, produceth many fcriptures, etc. . . . What fhould be the cause R. B. hath laboured fo much in this matter of dipping, and taken notice of every particular, I leave every man free to judge: for my part I take it to be, as I faid before: *It is new, and the man is mightily taken with it.* [He goes on to charge R. B. with] denying the Baptifme of all the Reformed Churches & separed [separated] Churches, & alfo of all other Chriftians, either Reformed, or yet in defection, only thofe *two or three* [Churches] excepted that have *within thefe two or three yeeres, or fome fuch fhort time, bin totally dipped* for Baptifme by perfons at the beginning unbaptized themfelves. [Further in referring to Barber's book, he cites his taunt: "the Church P. B. is a member of was unheard of till within these 200. yeeres," and replies] Well; two hundred yeeres is *fome* antiquitie, *more then two or three yeeres, fuch as is the defcent of the totall dippers in this kingdome.*

Here it will be noticed that the "very lately" of his book of April, 1642, becomes the more definite "two or three yeeres;" which, deducted from April, 1643, would fix the date of the origin of the practice of dipping, so far as his authority goes, as having been in 1640 or 1641. Another writer, J. Watts (1657), fourteen years later makes a statement which reaches nearly the same result: giving the origin of dipping in England — he probably wrote in 1656 — as "about 13. or 14. yeare agoe."[58]

---

[54] *The Second Part of the Vanity*, etc. [No. 10] p. 29.
[55] No. 168, p. 32.
[56] No. 13.
[57] *A Reply*, etc. [No. 18] pp. 19, 30, 31, 61.
[58] J. Watts, *A Scribe*, etc. [No. 219] p. 64.

To save space I shall now classify a number of corroborative testimonies, arranged in the order of their years of publication, viz.:

1644. D. FEATLEY. [59] — "this Article [the XLth of the *Anabaptift Confeffion* requiring dipping] is wholly fowred with *the new leaven* of Anabaptifme. I fay the *new leaven; for it cannot be proved that any of the ancient Anabaptifts maintained any fuch pofition.* . . . It is true, John baptized Chrift in Jordan, and Philip baptized the Eunuch in the river: but the text faith not, that either the Eunuch, or Chrift himfelf, or any baptized by John, or his Difciples, or any of Chrifts Difciples, were *dipped, plunged,* or *dowfed over head and ears,* as this Article implyeth, and our Anabaptifts *now* practife."

1644. W. COOKE: [60] "I would know with thefe *new Dippers,* whether the parties to be dowfed and dipped, may be baptized in a garment, or no? If they may, then happily [haply] the garment may keep the water from fome part of the body, and then they are not rightly baptized; for the whole man, fay they, muft be dipped."

1644. The author of the LOYALL CONVERT, etc. [61] styles this baptism by dipping: "*The New Distemper.*"

1644. I. KNUTTON: [62] "this opinion [of rebaptizing by dipping] being but *new and upftart,* there is good reason they should difclaime it, and be humbled for it."

1645. J. MABBATT [63] replies to Knutton's taunt not by denying, but by justifying, the newness, in saying: "the Apoftles were in their time charged for 'new and upftart' Doctrine by fome; fhould they by good reafon therefore difclayme it, and be humbled for it, and fo have denyed Chrifts doctrine and Truth," etc.

1645. E. PAGITT. [64] — "yea, at this day they [the Anabaptists] have a *new crotchet* come into their heads, that all that have not been plunged nor dipt under water, are not truely baptized, and thefe alfo they re-baptize . . . In the Thames and Rivers, the Baptizer, and the party baptized goe both into the Rivers, and the parties to be baptized are dipped or plunged under water."

1645. NINETEEN ARGUMENTS, etc.: [65] "The *new* Ordinance of Dipping," etc.

1645. J. SALTMARSH [66] calls "the *dipping* them in the water . . . the *new* Baptifm."

1645. HANSERD KNOLLYS, [67] in answering Saltmarsh, retorts that "Paul's Doctrine was called 'new,' although he preached Jefus and the Refurrection," etc.

1645. J. EACHARD [68] says: "the Anabaptiftes by a *new* baptifme . . . will not communicate with others, for they think they are more holy then others, by ftrictneffe of their order, etc."

1646. R. BAILLIE [69] declares: "Among the *new inventions* of the *late* Anabaptifts, there is none which with greater animofity they fet on foot, then [than] the neceffity of dipping over head and ears; then [than] the nullity of affufion and fprinkling in the adminiftra-

---

[59] *The Dippers Dipt,* etc. [No. 46] p. 187.
[60] *A Learned and Full Answer,* etc. [No. 30] p. 21.
[61] *The New Diftemper, written by the Author of the Loyall Convert,* etc. Oxford, 4°. pp. ii, 26. The whole book takes its name as an attack upon the "prophanations" of these dippers.
[62] *Seven Queftions,* etc. [No. 45] p. 23.
[63] *A Briefe or Generall,* etc. [No. 64] p. 32.
[64] *Herefiography,* etc. [No. 54] pp. 30, 31.
[65] No. 68, p. 4.
[66] *The Smoke in the Temple,* etc. [No. 69] pp. 15, 16.
[67] *The Shining of a Flaming Fire,* etc. [No. 74] p. 1.
[68] *The Axe Againft,* etc. [No. 75] p. 8.
[69] *Anabaptifm,* etc. [No. 102] p. 163.

[51]

tion of baptisme ... *The question about the necessity of dipping seems to be taken up onely the other year by the Anabaptists in England* ... The pressing of dipping, and exploding, of sprinkling, is but *an yesterday conceit* of the English Anabaptists ... Let us therefore consider if this *sparkle of new light* have any derivation from the lamp of the Sanctuary, etc."

1650. N. STEPHENS [70] argues: "If they [Anabaptists] say that the Commission Matt. xxviii: 19 was their first Administrators rule, then he must be a Disciple made by ordinary preaching and teaching, before he had authority to minister their *new* Baptisme."

1653. JOHN GOODWIN — the famous pastor of St. Stephens, Coleman St. — is a voluminous witness. He wrote three books within two years bearing upon the subject, and it would be wearisome to exhaust here the apt citations from these volumes. I extract a few as a sample.

From PHILADELPHIA, etc. (1653):[71] "the brethren of *new* Baptisme;" "the way of *new* Baptisme;" "surprised with a religious conceit of a necessity of *new* Baptisme;" "the children of *new* Baptisme," etc.

From WATER-DIPPING, etc. (1653):[72] "not simply lawful, but necessary also (in point of duty) for persons baptized *after the new mode of Dipping*, to continue communion with those churches ... of which they were members before the said Dipping;" "the *new mode of Dipping;*" "being actually baptized after the manner of the brethren of *new Baptisme;*" "the main Pillar upon which the house of our *new Dippers* of men, and dividers of Churches, is built;" "I heartily wish for the sake of some of them, whom I know, that their *new* Baptism doth not help to diminish their old grace;" "and for the Mode of the *latest and newest Invention* ... it is, as far as we are able to conceive by the representation of it made unto some of us, so contrived, and so to be managed, that the Baptist who dippeth according to it had need to be a man of stout limbs, and of a very able and active body: otherwise the person to be baptized, especially if in any degree corpulent, or unwieldy, runs a great hazard of meeting with Christs latter Baptism, instead of his former;" "persons baptized after the *new mode* of dipping."

From CATABAPTISM, etc. [73] (1655): "your *new* baptisme;" "after *the new mode of dipping;*" "Mr. W. A. himself in his 'Answer,' [App. No. 167] etc. maketh it matter of exception and complaint, that I sometimes stile my way of Rebaptizing *New Baptism*. And yet heretofore in discussing with a grave Minister of Mr. A's. judgement in the point of Rebaptizing, and the most ancient that I know walking in that way, finding him not so well satisfied that his way should be stiled Ana-baptism, I desired to know of him what other term would please him? His answer was *New Baptism;*" "and however Baptists of the *new order* abhominate the saying ... yet it may truly, at least beyond all reasonable contradiction be said that unto many, *their burying under water* hath hastened their burial also under earth."

1655. J. PARNELL [74] testifies: "now *within these late yeares* ... they [the Anabaptists] say ... they must be dipped in the water, and that they call baptising."

1657. J. WATTS [75] declares: "Dipping was, and is, as I have said, a *New business*, and a *very Novelty.*"

---

[70] *A Precept*, etc. [No. 137] p. 65.
[71] No. 166, pp. 13, 24, 25, 28.
[72] No. 169, pp. i, 5, 11, 26, 39, 89.
[73] No. 196, pp. vi, xxx, xxxii, 56.
[74] *The Watcher*, etc. [No. 202] p. 16.
[75] *A Scribe*, etc. [No. 219] p. iii.

1669. R. BAXTER:[76] "they [Anabaptists] do introduce a new fort of Chriftianity ... and a *new fort of Baptifm*, which the church of Chrift never knew to this day ... As if they were raifed in the end of the world to reform the Baptifm and Chriftianity of all ages, and were not only wifer than the univerfal church from Chrift till now, but alfo at laft muft make the Church another thing."

If these multiplied witnesses tell the truth, and the English Baptists, in or about 1641, did largely take up immersion as their form of administering baptism, in all human probability — since it would be too much to anticipate that the movement could instantly carry the convictions of the entire body — it must have resulted, that, for a time there were, side by side in that country, two sorts of Baptists; the one rejecting infant baptism, but using aspersion still, the other adding to their original tenet the fervent holding of the XLth Article of their creed of 1644. We are not without evidence that such was the fact. As late as 1660 we find *A Breife Defcription, or Character, of the Religion and Manners of the Phanatiques in Generall*, etc.[77] carefully distinguishing between simple Anabaptists, and *Dippers*. In 1656 the author of *Eirēnikon*[78] in undertaking to compose the existing theological differences of the time, thus speaks:

> But there are Anabaptifts — fo fome call them,
> Wee'l not Difpute the name: all good befall them.
> Good Brother, let thy Charity advance
> To give them *timeing* [the timing] of an Ordinance.
> And for what elfe moft hold, you need not fear them;
> However, 'tis not Chriftianlike to jeer them.
> *What though fome weak ones in the water fall?*
> Be modeft, Brother, do not cenfure all;
> Look but amongft them with impartial eyes
> You'll find ther's many godly, fober, wife.

I may be wrong, but I interpret the italicized line as referring to immersionists, as distinguished from their affusionist brethren. However this may be, we have a most square and definite testimony, in 1646,[79] to this effect, as to the town of Chelmsford, in Essex:

> It is fo filled with Sectaries, efpecially *Brownifts* and *Anabaptifts*, that a third part of the people refufe to communicate in the Church-Lyturgie, and halfe refufe to receive the bleffed Sacrament, unleffe they may receive it in what pofture they pleafe to take it. *They have amongft them two forts of Anabaptifts; the one they call the Old Men, or* ASPERSI, *becaufe they*

---

[76] *The Cure of Church-divifions; or Directions for weak Chriftians, to keep them from being Dividers or Troublers of the Church*, etc. 1669. 8°. pp. xlviii, 430, iv. [B. M. (873, i. 22.)] pp. 47, 48.

[77] No. 249, p. i.

[78] No. 214, p. 20.

[79] B. Ryves, *Mercurius Rufticus; or the Countries Complaint of the barbarous Out-rages committed by the Sectaries*. Oxford, 1646, sm. 8°. pp. xvi, 224. [B. M. [E. 1099. (1.)] p. 22.

[53]

were but *fprinkled: the other they call the New Men, or the* IMMERSI, *becaufe they were overwhelmed in their Rebaptization.*

One of my Baptist critics, after asking, in a mixture of indignation and triumph:[80] "When did English Baptist Churches cease to pour in baptism, and begin to immerse?" went on to say in censure of my intimation that such had been the case: "In this, as in other things, Dr. Dexter has allowed his eagerness in making out a case to overbear his fidelity as a historian." I now make respectful answer that — in my judgment — in view of the evidence I have herein presented, nothing but the obstinate and discreditable refusal to apply to matters touching his own denomination those principles and processes of reasoning which, with other men, he is accustomed to apply to all other things, can prevent a Baptist from conceding that the churches of his order in the mother country did introduce dipping, as a method of baptism at that time new, in or about the year 1641.

Before passing from the subject I desire to add a few words upon two related questions: Was there any truth in the ancient statements that the early English Baptists sent over to Holland in order to obtain genuine immersion thence? and that the ordinance was at first received by their candidates naked?

Crosby's view of the first matter seems to be that there were three ways possible for the recovery of the lost rite of immersion in England; viz.: (1) "that the firft adminiftrator fhould baptize himfelf, and then proceed to the baptizing of others;"[81] (2) "that firft they formed a church of their opinion in the point of baptifm; then the church appoints two of these minifters to begin the adminiftration of it, by baptizing each other; after this one, or both thefe, baptize the reft of the congregation;"[82] (3) "to fend over to the foreign Anabaptifts, who defcended from the antient Waldenfes in France or Germany, that fo one or more receiving baptifm from them, might become proper adminiftrators of it to others."[83] He says: "fome thought this [latter] the beft way, and acted accordingly;" but "the greateft number of the Englifh Baptifts, and

---

[80] The Chicago *Standard*, 1 July, 1880.
[81] *Hist Eng. Bap.* etc. i: 97.
[82] *Ibid.* i: 99. It is one of the curiosities of mental vagaries on such subjects, that it should never have occurred to the good people advocating this view, how illogical, upon their own principles, it was. They held that a true church which had not been entered by immersion was impossible; yet they proposed to form a church of unbaptized people, and to have that unbaptized church — which, being such, was no church, and had no church-power — exercise church-power enough to make ministers, and to authorize those ministers to immerse each other, and then to turn around and immerse the rest! With what consistency could such people in their next breath denounce pædobaptist churches as: "falfe churches, falfely conflituted in the baptifm of infants, and their own unbaptized eftate?"
[83] *Ibid.* i: 100.

the more judicious, looked upon all this as needlefs trouble, etc." [84] He himself was of opinion (1) that John Smyth had not baptized himself; and (2) that the English Baptists had not "derived their baptifm from the aforefaid Mr. Smith." [85] He therefore judged that most of the English Baptists received their immersion in the second way named. As we have seen, [86] he was further clear that Mr. Spilsbury had not sought foreign baptism. But he cites the Kiffin manuscript in proof that another Englishman did go abroad for that purpose.

The statement of the Kiffin paper is this: [87]

Several fober and pious perfons belonging to the congregations of the diffenters about London, were convinced that believers were the only proper fubjects of baptifm, and that it ought to be adminiftered by immerfion, etc. . . . They could not be fatiffyed about any adminiftrator in England to begin this practice; *becaufe tho' fome in this nation rejected the baptifm of infants, yet they had not, as they knew of, revived the antient cuftom of immerfion:* [88] But hearing that fome in the Netherlands practif'd it, they agreed to fend over one Mr. Richard Blount, who underftood the Dutch Language: That he went accordingly, carrying letters of recommendation with him, and was kindly received both by the church there, and Mr. *John Batte* their teacher: That upon his return, he baptized Mr. Samuel Blacklock, a minifter, and thefe two baptized the reft of their company, whofe names are in the manufcript, to the number of fifty-three.

Ivimey and Evans [89] appear to agree with Crosby in endorsing the trustworthiness of the account here given. On the other hand, had not Kiffin — as it is supposed — made the statement, it would be suspicious for its vagueness, and for the fact that none of the historians, not even Wilson, Calamy, Brook or Neal, know anything about either Blount or Blacklock, beyond what is here stated. It is true, however, that Edwards, [90] in 1646, speaks of "one *Blunt*, Emmes, and Wrighters Church" as "one of the firft and prime Churches of Anabaptifts now in thefe latter times;" and Barclay [91] seems to have discovered that there was a *John Batten*, who was "a well-known Collegiant, the teacher of a congregation of Collegiants at Leyden," whom he supposes to be the man who administered the immersion. Moreover, in 1676, E. Hutchinson, in speaking of the origin of the Baptists in England, says: [92]

The great objection was the want of an Adminiftrator, which (as I have heard) was removed by fending certain meffengers to *Holland,* whence they were fupplied.

---

[84] *Ibid.* i: 101.

[85] He was certainly in error as to Helwys and Murton, and the churches which they founded, and all who stood in succession from them.

[86] See p. 44, *ante.*

[87] *Hift. Eng. Bap.* i: 102.

[88] The reader will not fail to note the — incidental, and therefore influential — corroboration which this sentence affords to the demonstration already given that immersion was unknown to the Baptists in England between 1600 and 1641.

[89] *Hift. Eng. Bap.* etc. i: 145: *Early Eng. Bap.* etc. ii: 78.

[90] *Gangræna,* etc. 3d Pt. p. 112.

[91] *Inner Life,* etc. 75.

[92] *A Treatife,* etc. [No. 307] p. vi.

[55]

A broadside, which has been preserved in the library of the British Museum —bearing date 5 Jan. 1659—may perhaps be fairly taken in general corroboration of the Kiffin statement, although it refers to a previous attempt which was a failure in a more distant field. It purports to have been "written by a pious Gentleman that hath been thirteen yeares amongſt the Separatiſts."[93] He is describing Puritans who had become Anabaptists, and he says:

v. 11. Then you together took in hand
To build Chriſt houſe upon the ſand,
And ſtill you want the Corners-ſtone—
I mean Jeſus that is Chriſt alone.

v. 12. His word you know you did promiſe [peruse?]
And there you found the word baptize,
You ſaid the meaning of 't muſt be
Needs meant of water-Baptiſme.

v. 13. Then did you muſe and caſt your care
All for an Adminiſtrator;
But *here in England none was ſeen
That uſed aught but ſprinkling.*[94]

v. 14. At length you heard men ſay,
That there was Saints in *Sileſia*,
Who ever ſince the Apoſtles time
Had kept this Ordinance pure, divine.

v. 15. Thither alaſs you ſent in haſte
And thus you did ſome treaſure waſte,
But when your meſſengers came there
They were deceiv'd as we are here.

v. 16. But this they told you in good deed,
That *they* of baptiſm ſtood in need;
And for a preſent remedy,
With prayers they to Heaven did cry.

v. 17. Then did they with a joynt conſent
Do that of which you now repent,
Authorize one them to baptize
Thus this fine cheat they did deuiſe.

. . . .

v. 19. And thus, at length, you yourſelves baptized,
Till you another ſect deuiſed;
etc.   etc.   etc.   etc.

---

[93] *Antiquakeriſm, or a Character of the Quakers Spirit from its Original*, etc. [No. 238.]

[94] Another incidental proof of the truth of the main argument of this chapter.

The same sheet contains a marginal *prose* note, thus:

> They fent up and down the world for a man to baptize them, but they found none, but fuch as had baptized themfelves. In *England* there was fome [kindred spirits, *i.e.* Baptists] in the practice of fprinckling,[94] but thefe the Dippers, to my knowledge, did reject from communion with them on this very ground.

From all which it seems safe to conclude that while Mr. Blount probably did go to Holland and obtain immersion from the *Collegianten*, this was the only case of the sort, and did not alter the fact that the majority of the Calvinistic Baptists of England originated immersion among themselves, after the second manner which Crosby suggests.

The testimony as to the remaining question is conflicting. We may most intelligently glance at this also in chronological order; and I shall assume that the truth of the old maxim *fas eſt ab hoſte doceri*, will sufficiently cover the point of some value in the evidence of those who did not agree with, and even maligned these men, to make it worth our while to include in aid of our judgment two or three specimens of what they said.

1643. AN ANABAPTISTS SERMON, etc.[95] This word waſh ... is not to fprinkle them with a little idolatrous water out of a Font or Bafon; but to powre water on their heads; nay to dip them in water over head and eares; for fuch dipping will fetch the faltneſſe of finne out of their natures ... Unleſſe all be thus rebaptized *ſtark naked*, & diped as well head as tayle, as you are, none can be faved.

1644. THE ANABAPTISTS GROUND-WORK, etc.[96] I aſk T.[homas] L.[amb] and the reſt of thoſe Baptiſts, or Dippers, that will not be called Anabaptiſts (though they baptize fome that have been twice baptized before[97]) what rule they have by word or example in Scripture, *for their going men and women together into the water*, and for their manner of dipping, and every circumſtance and action they perform concerning the fame.

1644. D. FEATLEY.[98] The refort of great multitudes of men and women together in the evening, and *going naked into rivers*, there to be plunged and Dipt, cannot be done without fcandall ... They ſtrip themfelves *ſtark naked*, ... when they flock in great multitudes, men and women together, to their Jordans to be dipt, etc.

1644. S. RICHARDSON[99] answering Featley, says: Wee anfwer, wee abhor it [baptism naked] and deny that any of us ever did fo, and challenge him to prove it againſt us, if he can.

1645. THE ANABAPTISTS CATECHISME, etc.:[100]
    Q. *Why are you called Anabaptiſts?*

---

[95] No. 19, pp. 5, 8.
[96] No. 24, p. 23.
[97] Notice the confirmation here further given of the fact that the Baptists before 1641, or thereabouts, had been *aſſuſed* as adults. Only so could their ultimate immersion become the *third* administration of the rite to them.
[98] *The Dippers Dipt, etc.* [No. 46] pp. 36, 167.
[99] *Some Brief Considerations*, etc. [No. 48] p. 5.
[100] No. 59, p. 1.

A. Becaufe we went *naked* into the pure water, and were dipped in the holy ftreames, where we clenfed our bodies (from the corruption that was before upon us) in the prefence of the Brethren, and the Sifters of the Congregation.

1645. T. EDWARDS collected feveral teftimonies in the drag-net of his *Gangræna:* [101] They [the Anabaptifts] have baptized many weakly antient women *naked* in rivers in winter, whereupon fome have fickened and died ... In baptizing women *naked* in the preter ce and fight of men ... No wonder he [a man of doubtful reputation become Anabaptift preacher] and many fuch, turned Dippers *to dip young maids and young women naked,* for it was the fitteft trade to ferve their turns that could be ... A company of uncleane men under the pretence of Religion, might have thereby faire opportunities to feed their eyes full of adultery in *beholding young women naked,* and in *handling young women naked,* being about them in dreffing and undreffing them, etc. ... Many in our times who profeffed Religion were luftfull filthy perfons, though this was covered under a profeffion of Religion, and therefore fo foon as they heard of an opinion of baptizing grown perfons, and that *by dipping of naked women,* they prefently fell to it, as the beft way to enjoy their lufts by, etc.[102]

1646. THE TIMES DISPLAYED [103] [represents the Anabaptift as saying]:

> After fo long a night of woe and forrow
> Behold a fair, and a delicious morrow;
> After fo many years, when we oppreft
> Were fined, imprifoned, and could never reft,
> For the Beafts Image, the hated Bifhops, now
> We openly and without dread avow
> Our tenets, dipping maids and wives each day
> Their natural concupicence to allay;
> And although fome we drown, thofe drowned fo
> Doe but by water unto heaven goe.

1648. R. ALLEN [104] argues: If it be fufficient reafon againft Infant Baptifm that there is no exprefs precept or example for it, then let the Anabaptifts themfelves for fhame leave off that *fhameful ftripping and dipping* their profelytes, or elfe fhew me where they have any exprefs command or example for it ... As for their *ftripping,* it is againft common honefty and modefty, and that dipping is not neceffary to be ufed, is clear from their own argument, becaufe they have no where one exprefs word of command or warrant for it.

1650. T. BAKEWELL: [105] Neither may they have garments for that use [of dipping] confecrated as Aarons breeches, Exod. 28 : 42, 43. This would be as bad as the Prelates Surpleffs; and for women to wear them, being mans apparel, it were an abomination to the Lord, Deut. 22 : 5.

---

[101] No. 76, pp. 67, 143; No. 99, pp. 189, 261.

[102] *Edwards* elsewhere [p. 55] adds a confirmatory incident:

Another woman having a defire to be Re-baptized, and having pulled off all her cloaths to the naked fkin, ready to go into the Water, but forbearing during the time the Dipper prayed, fhe covered her fecret parts with both her hands; the which the Dipper efpying, told the woman that it was an unfeemly fight to fee her hold her hands downward, it being an Ordinance of Iefus Chrift, her hands, with her heart, fhould be lifted upwards toward heaven (as he fhow'd her how he did), but fhe, refufing for modefties fake, could not be Re-baptifed.

[103] *The Times Difplayed, in Six Seftyads: the firft a Prefbyter and an Independent; the fecond an Anabaptift and a Brownift,* etc. 4°. pp. 24. [D. M. (E. 365. [10.])] p. 8.

[104] *An Antidote,* etc. [No. 121] pp. 122, 125.

[105] *Doctor Chamberlen vifited,* etc. [No. 134] p. 20.

1652. T. HALL:[106] Now it cannot be imagined that John and the Apostles having great multitudes present at their baptism, would thus Dip *men and women stark naked* (or as some of our Anabaptists, *next to naked*) against the Rules of Modesty and Civility.

1653. II. HAGGAR:[107] I believe I have baptized and been at the baptizing of many hundreds, if not thousands, and *never saw any baptized naked in my life*, neither is it allowed nor approved of amongst any that I know of. But suppose that some men have been baptized naked, when there were none but men together, would this be such an unheard of wickedness?

1653. J. GOODWIN:[108] Besides, we do not read in the Scriptures of any Baptismal Boots, or Baptismal Breeches, or of shifting garments to avoyd the danger of being baptized, or of *encircling women with women after their coming from the water to salve their modesty*, with some other devices now, or of late, in frequent use amongst our *new* Baptists in the way of their practise.

1653. W. ERBURY:[109] Lastly let the world judge if the modesty of Gospel churches would suffer so many *naked women* to be dipt with men.

1657. J. WATTS:[110] By this time, Sir, I hope you see that your dipping of women in their clothes is a new business in the church, and hath no print or footsteps to be seen in the old way, or amongst the ancient Writers and Fathers of the former churches. Yea, this your clothes-dipping also, is so new a thing, that not much above fourteen or fifteen years ago your predecessors, and primer Anabaptists, the Virgins of Sion, and the precious Sons of the same, the proselytes of those dayes, did in the Evening resort and run together, and went *naked* into the Rivers, their Jordan, and were there dipped and plunged *in their naked bodies (without clothes on them)* by their John Dippers, or Dipper-Johns . . . Your ancient fathers did not dip in your manner, nor is it [your manner] as old as your elder Brothers, who about 13. or 14. yeare ago, ran about the country; for they did not dip in your manner, in their clothes, *but naked*.

1658. A. HOUGHTON:[111] It is neither full nor pertinent to the interrogatory [he is referring to the denial of H. Haggar above (1653)]; you speak *to the naked dipping*, but not to *next to naked* . . . and *if the beholding men and women in their shirts*, etc. be not a coasting upon incivility, I have lost my understanding.

I add but a single further witness, and he of some years later: one who will hardly be suspected of scant information, or the disingenuous use of facts:

1675. R. BAXTER:[112] In the year 1647, or 1648, or both, when Anabaptistry began suddenly to be obtruded with more successful fervency than before, I lived near Mr. Tombes, in a country where some [Anabaptists] were, and within the hearing of their practice in other parts of the land: And that in that beginning the common fame of Ministers and people was, that in divers places *some baptized naked, and some did not:* and that I never to my best remembrance heard man or woman contradict that report till this man [Mr. D'Anvers] did it in this writing. And that no Anabaptist contradicted it to me that I then

---

[106] *The Collier in his Colours*, etc. [B. M. (E. 658. [2.])] p. 115.
[107] *The Foundation of the Font*, etc. [No. 164] p. 102.
[108] *Water-Dipping*, etc. [No. 169] p. 40.
[109] *The Madmans Plea*, etc. [No. 181] p. 6.
[110] *A Scribe, Pharisee*, etc. [No. 219] pp. 20, 64.
[111] *An Antidote*, etc. [No. 221] p. 266.
[112] *More Proofs of Infant Church-Membership*, etc. [No. 299] pp. 282, 283.

or since conversed with: And that thereupon in 1659, I wrote against both sorts — those that *baptized naked*, and those that did not: And after all this when Mr. Tombes answered my book, *and those very passages*, he *never denied the truth of the thing* (though he did not so baptize himselfe) ... and I appeal to impartial reason whether he would not then at the time have denied it, had it been deniable ... I must confesse *I did not see the persons baptized naked*, nor do I take it to be lawfull to defame any upon doubtful reports: But when it is a *fame common*, and *not denied by themselves*, either ministers or people at the time, I think it is to be taken so much notice of as the confuting of the evil doth require. I know not by sight that there is a Fornicator, Adulterer, Murderer, or Thief (as I remember) in England: And yet if I neither Write nor Preach to call such to repentance left I be a slanderer in saying that there are any such, I think it would be foolish uncharitable charity, and unrighteous justice.

I leave my readers to draw their own inferences from this testimony; freely confessing that to my mind the best solution of its contradictions is found in the theory that there were, in the beginning of immersion in England, Baptists and Baptists; that, very likely, in those rude and turbulent times, there may have been some among them who were fanatical, and some who were destitute of all delicacy of feeling; possibly some scoundrels masquerading in the garb of piety for the service of their lusts; and that Mr. Baxter was quite right in concluding that "some baptized naked, and some did not." Very possibly also there may have been at times room for honest misapprehension, inasmuch as the garments sometimes worn appear to have been so scanty, that, to a spectator on the bank of the stream, the candidate when partly immersed might appear to be wholly unclad. And I construe the note in the margin of the fortieth Article of the Anabaptist Creed of 1644 which I have cited,[113] as corroborative of this view; being intended as much on the one hand to repress undesirable license among their own people, as, on the other, to convince outsiders of the propriety of their way.

I shall close this chapter by two or three further extracts which seem to me worth publicity, for the light which they cast upon some aspects of the general subject.

In Watts's *Scribe*,[114] etc. (1657) he gives a brief statement of the *modus operandi* of the late baptism of two women which had been furnished him by some Baptist hand — to the effect that the two women privately changed their clothes, and went into the water above the knees; that the administrator tied their clothes about their knees with a string, and dipped them over head and ears; and that they then went out of the water and shifted themselves, with the help of some of the sisters.

---

[113] See p. 41.   [114] No 219, p. v.

We get a much more circumstantial account, in 1646, in the pages of *Mercurius Civicus*,[115] which is as follows:

We have been importuned to give you the relation of the rebaptizing of a woman at *Hempsted* in *Hartfordshire*, in a river called *Bourn End*, hard by *Bourn Mill:* which, to shew the strangenes of the manner, and the madnesse of that Sect, we have here inserted, as from authenticke hands it was sent unto us.

In the Parish of Hempsted in Hartfordshire [116] there liveth one *James Browne*, by trade a Sawyer; by calling a converter of holy sisters; by person of a very big and tall stature; by Religion formerly a good Protestant, diligent in hearing of sermons, and alwayes seeking to hear the best men. Now of late time, within these six or seaven yeares,[117] he hath quite left the Church; and instead of hearing of Gods Ministers in publique, he is become a preacher and teacher of others (especially of women) going about from house to house preaching and teaching, Instructing and Baptizing; (or Rebaptizing) doing good as they say to so many as adhere to his kinde of Teaching: and he is either the second or third man of note for spirituall abilities (as the Brethren are pleased to call them) in all that part of the Country.

About the middle of September now last past, 1646, this *James Browne*, having on a day Preached (or as they call it spoken) unto an assembly of the Brethren, where he inveighed against Baptizing of Infants; affirming it to be a most damnable popish sinne: and that all true Christians ought more to mourne and lament for that they were Baptized when they were Infants, then for all the sinnes that ever they committed in the whole course of their lives; and further shewing how necessary and needful it was to salvation (having attained unto a sufficient measure of Faith) to be rebaptized. One *Mary Halsey*, wife of *William Halsey*, a holy woman of the company, desired to be baptized a new: showing her selfe to be very sorrowful for the blindnesse of her parents, that would have her Baptized in her Infancy, before she knew what it meant, and she (being then without Faith) unworthy of it. *Browne* having throughly examined this his new Convert, and found her to have attayned to a competent knowledge, the examination ended.

This woman with *Browne* went into a River, neere hand to the house of that dayes exercise called *Bourne End* River; and there, neere unto *Bourne End* Mill, in a place of the River somewhat deeper then the ordinary Channell, where having joyned together they went down into the water: *Browne* went down in his leather Breeches in which he used to go to Sawing: and the woman went into the water in a paire of Linnen Drawers onely to cover her Shame; made of purpose for such like uses; the rest of her body being all quite naked.

In this water, *Browne* washed her body all over from top to toe, rubbing her with his hands, as men do their sheep when they wash them; and so clensed her from all filthinesse (as he saith, both of body and spirit) and throwing water upon her, used the words of Baptisme: *I Baptize thee, in the name of the Father, and of the Sonne, and of the Holy Ghost:* thrusting her head three times into the water because three persons in Trenity: and in this water I wash and purge away all thy sinnes; sending them down the stream, together with this water that runneth off thy body: so that now thou art made as cleane again from all sinne and wickednesse as ever thou wast in thy Infancy: nay, cleaner, for now thy originall sinne if thou hadst any, is

---

[115] *Mercurius Civicus*, Oct. 8-15, 1646. [B. M. (E. 357 [12.])] p. 2414.

[116] *Ivimey* [ii: 178] mentions Hemel Hempstead in Herts as the seat of an ancient Baptist church, probably founded "about the period of the Revolution," but says nothing of Browne in connection with it.

[117] Note how all these time references date back very nearly to the same period.

quite taken away, and thou art now received into the number of Chrifts chofen Children; and made a member of his Myfticall body, and mayeft be fully affured of the Kingdome of Heaven.

This being done, they departed out of the water, and went to the place of that dayes exercife.

This was feen and heard by the Miller of *Bourne End*, and fome others, who had got behind a hedge to heare and fee the action. As they were going out of the water, the Miller called to them, and wifhed *Browne* to rub her a little more; for there is (faith he) I doubt one fpot that is not yet made white; and they departed making no anfwer, and a man with them, that the woman brought doune with her to look to her apparell, which fhe put off neere the River fide when fhe went into the water.

It so happens that we have remaining a tract which had its origin in the very company out of whose amicable separation grew the first Calvinistic Baptist English church, and which lets us in to the exact nature of the differences then under discussion between different portions of that body as to Baptism. It was written about ten years after the division by which Mr. Spilsbury's church was formed, and its references to dipping seem to me to imply such newness in that discussion, as to corroborate the theory that Mr. Spilsbury at first affused his adult believers. It is entitled *To Sions Virgins: or a fhort forme of Catechifme of the Doctrine of Baptifme. In ufe in thefe times that are fo full of Queftions. By an antient member of that long agoe gathered Congregation whereof Mr. Henry Jacob was an Inftrument of gathering it, and the Paftour worthy of double honour, Mr. John Lathropp fucceeding him, now paftor in New England*, etc. Printed in the yeare 1644."[118] Two or three extracts from its pages will show us precisely how the debate was then proceeding. Beginning by asserting and advocating Infant Baptism, with various particulars, it asks:[119]

Q. *What forme is to be ufed in baptifme?*
A. The Minifter is to dip his hand, and to powre cleane water, fprinkle and wafh the finner, and fo it is fully baptifed.

Q. *Is not dipping of the head full baptifme?*
A. No, not without powring, fprinkling, and wafhing; no more then giving whole wafers in the fupper: there was bread, but no breaking fhewing forth Chrifts fufferings; fo whole rivers fhewes not forth Chrifts fufferings, powring Him out like water befprinkling all His rayment.

Q. *What is it for the finners to goe into the water themfelves, and come out themfelves to fhew forth death and buriall?*
A. A lying figne, to make a figure of the creature, for wee muft fee Chrift in the imployment of the Officer, and ufe of the Water, powring, fprinkling, wafhing: there muft bee a dipper dipping his hand, but not a dipped, but in Chrift himfelfe who by his owne power puts into himfelfe the Rocke and fountaine.

---

[118] No. 36.   [119] p. 2.

[62]

Q. What speakes powring out of water? [120]
A. (1) It speakes Christ poured out like water. (2) It speakes Christ powring out cleane water upon beleevers washing away filth. (3) It speakes powring out of the spirit, so that out of the belly of believers may flow rivers of water of life.

Q. What speakes washing?
A. It speakes washing from filthinesse and clensing from sin.

Q. What speakes sprinkling?
A. (1) It speakes sprinkling the conscience from dead works. (2) It speakes our high calling, being called to the blood of sprinkling.

· · · · · · · · ·

Q. What doth Christ teach beleevers by powring water on the baptized — Infants or other? [121]
A. Christ teacheth beleevers to power out their soules to him, hee having powred out His Spirit upon them giving them power to be His Sonnes and Daughters, so there is [as?] great use to eye Christ in the use of the ordinance as once to be baptized.

Q. What is held forth of Christ in dipping the Baptized?
A. To dip an Infant there is a dim light of Christ, as in the whole wafer no shewing forth Christ his suffering: but for a creature to goe in and out of the water, the dipper to dip downe the head, is no shewing Christ at all as I can see. I have not so learned Christ.

· · · · · · · · · ·

Let them take heede that teach these "new truths" as they call them, these *new forms*,[123] or newly taken up.[122]

I do not see how a candid reading of the multiplied authorities here presented, can fail to justify the conclusions which I have drawn.

---

[120] *Ibid.* p. 2.   [121] *Ibid.* p. 5.   [122] *Ibid.* p. 7.
[123] Notice the corroboration here (1644) afforded to the general argument of this chapter, making dipping a new form in or about 1641.

CHAPTER III.

SOME CONSIDERATION OF THE HISTORICAL VALUE OF THE ALLEGED "ANCIENT RECORDS" OF THE BAPTIST CHURCH OF CROWLE, ETC.

THE *General Baptist Magazine* of London, in its issue for July, 1879, published an article entitled "The Beginnings of Liberty,"[1] which was largely made up of extracts from what purported to be the ancient records of the "Church of Chrift meeting at Epworth, Crowle, and Weft Butterwick," in Lincolnshire, Eng. A second article, in the October number of the same journal for the same year, entitled "John Norcott,"[2] contained a few additional extracts.[3] The quality of these was so remarkable as speedily to attract attention on this side of the Atlantic; inasmuch as, if to be depended upon for stating the truth, they would go far to modify not merely the accepted annals of Nonconformity in the old country, but those of the Plymouth Colony as well.

The Baptist and other religious journals of England appear to have received these "quotations" without question as genuine and trustworthy, and I have heard that Mr. Spurgeon has on one or two occasions made them his authority for some public utterance. One Baptist gazette in this country referred to them as settling certain controverted questions "beyond reasonable dispute;"[4] but most of the American newspapers of that denomination so far as I observed touched them gingerly, if at all. Meanwhile, although it was vaguely stated[5] that these "ancient records" had been submitted to an "antiquarian," who, after examination, had "certified his belief that they are genuine, and refer to the days of Queen Elizabeth;" no historical scholar in England appeared to think the matter of sufficient consequence to make such a thorough examination at first hand, and on the ground, as might furnish a

---

[1] *General Baptist Magazine for 1879. Edited by John Clifford, M.A. LL.B., B Sc., Fellow of the Geological Society. The Eighty-First Volume.* London, E. Marlborough & Co. 51 Old Bailey. 8°, pp. 500, p. 327.
[2] *Ibid.* p. 438.
[3] The London *Baptist* of 6 Feb. 1880, I have seen it stated also contained the same, or similar, extracts; but I have never met with that paper.
[4] The Hartford *Christian Secretary*, 4 Aug. 1880.
[5] This statement was made in the *Christian Secretary*, of the above date, apparently having been copied from the London *Baptist*. I find nothing of the sort mentioned in the *General Baptist Magazine*.

reasonable basis for their acceptance as authentic data by the student of those times.

Anxious, in the absence of all more competent endeavor, to do what I could for my own satisfaction in the matter, on 6 May last, I went up from London on purpose to get a look, if possible, at these venerable papers. Crowle is a little market town and parish of Lincolnshire, near the confluence of the Trent and the Ouse; containing a few more than 3,000 inhabitants, and easily reached by rail from Doncaster, from which it is distant some fifteen miles in a direction a little north of east. I was so fortunate as to find the Rev. Jabez Stutterd, who is the pastor of the General Baptist Church in that place, and the copyist of the documents in question, at home, and was very kindly received by him. On telling him the purpose of my visit, and asking to be permitted, under his supervision, to examine the original ancient manuscript, I was grieved — more, I will confess, than surprised — to be told that that original has been for some time lost, — it is feared irrecoverably, — and that only his copy remains. This copy he assured me that he made, with all possible care, *about fifteen years* before. This he was very willing I should transcribe in full, and in the most obliging manner aided me to do so. I found several passages to be included which have never been printed; some of them, if possible, of a more extraordinary character than any heretofore made public. I now proceed to give the whole consecutively, with Mr. Stutterd's appended voucher for the fidelity of my work.

I should premise here, that, in the matter of spelling, I found considerable variation in different portions of these extracts; owing, perhaps to Mr. Stutterd's failure always, as to that, to follow closely his original. I have therefore, throughout, in this respect conformed to the style of orthography indicated in those parts which partake most strongly of the characteristics of the date assigned to them.

The first Church Covenant — 4 January, 1599.

Wee, this Church of Chrift (meeting at Epworth, Crowle and Weft Butterwick, in ye County of Lincoln) whofe names are underwritten, give up ourfelues to ye Lord, and one to another, according to ye will of God, and do promife and covenant in ye prefence of Chrift, to walke together in ye lawes and ordinances of baptized belieuers, according to ye rules of ye gofpel, through Jefus Chrift. He helping us.

James Rayner,
Henry Helwife,   ⎫
John Morton,   ⎬ *Elders of*
William Brewfter,   ⎭ *ye Church.*
William Bradford,

[32 signatures, or marks.]

1598, 20 November. William Bradford baptized in ye old river Torne, below Epworth town, at midnight. Moon fhone bright. To God bee praife euermore.[6]

1603, 3 September. Our poor people are hunted & persequted on every fide: fome taken & fhut up in prifons.

Things have come to fuch a paffe among us it has been refolved, yet not without a bitter ftruggle on our parts as a Church of Chrift meeting at Crowle, Epworth & Butterwick, that for the fake of peace we fhall leaue this our dear native countrye & retire to Holland, wher, we heare, there is freedome of religion for all men. Wee fhall haue to learne a newe language, and get our liuings we know not how. It is a dear place & fubject to ye mifferies of warre: is thought by many of ye brethren, an adventure almoft defperate, a cafe intolerable, & a mifferie worfe then death. Efpetially feeing our brethren are not acquainted with trads nor traffique (by which Hollanders fubfifte) but wee are ufed to plaine countrie life and farming.

Wee have refolued to pray vnceafinglie: our chiefe difficultie is wee cannot ftay, yet wee are not fuffered to goe; for ye Ports & Hauens are fhut againft us, fo wee muft looke for fecrete meanes of conveyance, fee ye failers, & pay high rates for our paffage.

1603, 3 November. Brother Brewfter found a fea-captaine who agreed to take us from Bofton in this county to Amfterdam in Holland. Wee parted with our goods, repaired to Bofton as fecretly as wee could. Wee arrived before ye captaine, & had a wearie time waiting, fearing wee might bee betrayed. The veffel appeared at night. Wee embarked with our goods, & now thought — furely the bitterneffe of death is paft. But, no, the fhip was borded by ferchers, & other officers, with whom our Captaine was in league. In ye deade of ye night wee were turned out into open boats, & fearched & ranfaked by ye officials — women as wel as men. When they had taken all our money, bookes & goods from us, they carried us before ye mageftrates, who ordered us off to prifon, where we lay for a month: our only crime being that we would worfhip God in liberty of confcience.

The monthe after the greater number of us 72. were releafed; but Mr. Brewfter & feaven others were detained & conveyed to Lincoln goale, to bee tryed at the Affizes. Wee trudged homewards to Crowle, Butterwick, Epworth, where wee arrived pennyleffe, hungrie and tired: but ye brethren met for prayer.

1603, 30 December. The judge at Lincoln Affizes has been more merciful than wee dared to hope. Our brethren & fifters are fet at libertie. But thefe perfequtions are unendurable. Wee have firmly refolved to make another effort to departe.

1604, 12 February. John Smith, Vicar of Gainfborough, came inquiring about our views: he debated nearly all night with Elders Henry Helwife and John Morton, who defended our caufe well. Hee comes againe in a fhort time.

1604, 7 May. John Smith has carefully read ye fcriptures and is convinced wee are in ye truth: hee tells us he was deceived in ye way of Pædobaptiftry, & does now embrace ye fayth in ye true Chriftian & Apoftolic baptifme.

Hee difcourfed fweetly laft night in Elder James Rayners chamber from "Lo, ye kingdom of God is within you." It was fweet as honie. He will refigne his church living, & ye Church

---

[6] This entire entry about Bradford is not in Mr. Stutterd's manufcript copy, which merely bears a marginal endorsement of Bradford's immersion at this date. I transcribe this therefore from the printed verfion in the *Magazine*; Mr. S. attefting the genuineness of that.

[66]

of Chrift at Epworth, wnich hee fays is ye true Church of Chrift, will receive him for baptifme.

1606, 24 March. This night at midnight Elder John Morton baptized John Smith, vicar of Gainfborough in the river Don. It was fo dark wee were obliged to have torch-lights. Elder Brewfter prayed, & Mr. Smith made a good confeffion. Walked to Epworth in his cold clothes, but received no harm. The diftance was over two miles. All our friends were prefent. A ftrong wind, but faire aboue-head. To ye triune God be all ye praife.

1607, 10 February. John Smith has held filent meetings at midnight all this week at Brigg, Beltoft, Epworth, Butterwick. At Crowle ye parifh parfon told us hee would informe. William Bradford is to holde fourth next Tuefday at Crowle Croffe.

1607, 16 February. William Bradford, from Aufterfield, wifhed to fpeake at Crowle Croffe, but ye parfon prevented him, & flogged him with his horfe-whip, & fet his bull-dogge at him; but hee awed ye brute off with his ftaffe.

1609, 22 March. Wee kept a folemn daye of prayer. The Church had fmall communion for fome monthes till God put it into our hearts to humble ourfelves, reforme his houfe, and fett upon his work almofte loft by fix yeares perfeqution.

1609, 24 March. John Norcott, of Crowle, baptifed at two of ye clocke in ye morn, in ye river Torne, by John Smith, late Vicar of Gainfborough. [7]

1609, 30 March. A meeting of ye Church to-night. John Smith, late vicar of Gainfborough, John Morton, Henry Helwife, Richard Carver, William Bradford, James Rayner, William Brewfter, Eli Kelfey, John Rowe,[8] met to confult on removing ye Church into Holland on account of perfeqution.[9] They refolved to remove part of ye Church into Holland in order to ye quiet enjoyment of ye ordinances of his houfe in Apoftolic manner. Lord, doe help us.[10]

1609, 4 April. Received at ye Supper of ye Lord John Norcott. John Smith broke ye bread & mingled ye wine in James Rayners apple-chamber. John Norcott chofe as ye Elder of ye Church.[11]

1609, 4 April. Rev. John Smith ftarted in an open boat from Butterwick down ye Trent river unto Hull, thence to Holland (Ghent or Leyden) to enjoy liberty of confcience in a foreign country. John Norcott, Henry Helwife, John Morton, Richard Carver, William Bradford went. More are to followe.

John Carver,
William Bradford,
Thomas Prince,
Edward Winflow,
} Elders.[12]

---

[7] This entire entry I did not find in Mr. Stutterd's copy, but I insert it here as having been printed in the *General Baptist Magazine* [1879, p. 439], and therefore, a further extract of like authenticity with its companions, so attested by Mr. S.

[8] This name is printed John *Wood* in the *General Baptist Magazine* [1879, p. 439], where the extract is given.

[9] To this extract as printed above in the *Gen. Bap. Mag.* are added the names of "James Rayner, William Brewfter and John Morton — *Elders.*" The date *there* named for this entry is *4 April, 1609*.

[10] This last entry beginning at "They refolved," etc. is not in Mr. Stutterd's copy, but is printed as above, as being duly copied from the record.

[11] The same is true of this entire passage.

[12] I was a little doubtful as to the significance of these four names thus appended, but Mr. Stutterd said that he understood it as an official certificate inserted in the body of the record to authenticate the same.

1613. John Rowe has come home from Holland, and fays our friends haue no peace. The baby-baptifers are verily mad. John Norcott has written his book on baptifm, and got it printed. And he [John Rowe] has brought one with him home. It is quaint, but according to yᵉ Bible.

1614, December. Thomas Petch has returned very unwell from Holland, and brings yᵉ fad newes of yᵉ fudden deaths of John Smith & John Norcott of putrid fever, after a few houres illnefs. They were both buried in one graue. Their confolations in Chrift were wonderful. In life united — in death not diuided.

1615, February. John Carver, William Bradford, Edward Winflow, William Brewfter, Richard Carver, John Morton, Henry Helwife, John Turner, Thomas Tinker, Samuel Fuller, Edward Fuller, John Oldham, returned from Holland. Oh how dejected! Poore deare foules!

1615, 16 March. John Morton, William Bradford, goue over to Collingham and Mifterton to confult Elder Warner of Mifterton, and put thinges in order. Thinges diforderly at both places.

1617, November. The Church Elders refolved to day to fell their eftates & move from England to provinces lately difcovered by Sir Walter Raleigh in Virginia. Continual haraffment by Ecclefiaftical Courtes and Bifhops Mandamufes. Six of our friends are in Lincoln gaole, charged with reading the Word, & praying themfelves, in ftead of going to church to publique prayers.

1617, 10 November. John Morton returned from Chichefter where he went as foon as he came home from Holland, to fet things orderly there.

1617, ———. John Morton fell ficke and dyed. Buried at Butterwick in yᵉ front of yᵉ meeting door. A good man. Hee were twice in Lincoln Old Caftle. Hee was a bright light. May his wēry bones reft peacefull.

1618, 1 January. Agree to hold a faft day & much prayer for yᵉ poor deare foules in Lincoln gaole. Doe Lord hear us when wee crie.

1619. John Carver, Richard Carver, William Bradford, Edward Winflow, William Brewfter, John Turner, Thomas Tinker, Samuel Fuller, & Edward Fuller, fold yʳ eftates & decided to goe to Merica, or wee fhall foon be in gaole. Oh, thefe fiery perfequtors!

1620, 22 July. Hired a fhallop to ftart for Bofton Deepes, there one met us to take us on to Plimoth. The church met all night this night for folemn prayer and farewel. Oh yᵉ sobs & yᵉ fighes & groaninges in yᵉ fpirit. Seventy-four of us moving away.

Agreed by the Church not to haue no commune with Robinfon, and not any of that party, Becaufe wee beleeue:
I. Jefus Chrift dyed for all human kinde.
II. Yᵉ Holy Ghoft renewes mans fallen ftates.
III. Wee baptife man & woman; not babys.

William Bradford,
Enoch Clapham,
Edward Fuller,
Edward Winflow,
William Brewfter,
Thomas Tinker.[13]

---

[13] Mr. Stutterd's explanation with regard to these names was the same as that before given in a similar case: "They seemed to be affixed to authenticate the record."

[68]

CERTIFICATE OF AUTHENTICATION.

I hereby certify that, in the year 1866, several loose leaves of the original church records of the Ancient Baptist Church of Crowle, Epworth and Butterwick, came into my possession, and were copied by me with great care; and that the above transcript [14] *by Mr. Dexter, has this day been by him made in my presence from my copy then taken, and, according to my best knowledge and belief, is faithful to those originals, now lost.*

[Signed] *Jabez Stutterd*
General Baptist Minister
Crowle Lincoln,
May. 6th 1881.

Had these "extracts" been first printed *in full*, as above, on the American side of the Atlantic, they could have awakened little more than a passing wonder as to what manner of man should have taken the trouble of their origin; and would scarcely have been thought worthy of serious examination — least of all of deliberate refutation. But the critical study of the beginnings of Nonconformity seems to be now so much less common in England than in America, that these amazing declarations — at least such and so many of them as were then made public — appear at once to have gained unquestioning acceptance there, as a genuine and valuable addition to the sources of Separatist history. Twice, at least, the literary editor of the *Nonconformist and Independent*[15] has cited them as if they stood on a par in point of authority with Winthrop's or Pepys's Journal, or Bradford's and Strype's Histories; while one of the freshest issues of the London press — a volume called *The English Baptists, Who They are, and What they have done*, etc.[16] — founds upon their statements in regard to John Smyth an important portion of its argument and appeal. It seems to be needful, therefore, to give them a consideration to which in themselves they have no claim, and this must plead my apology for

---

[14] Mr. Stutterd referred me to the extracts which had been published in the *General Baptist Magazine*, as being authentic, except as he then and there amended them in one or two slight particulars; so that this voucher covers all the extracts here given, whether actually copied from Mr. S's manuscript, or copied from the *Magazine* under his eye.

[15] In its issues of 30 Sept. 1880, and 18 Aug. 1881.

[16] Edited by John Clifford, M.A., LL.B., and published by E. Marlborough & Co., 1881.

repeating here the offense which has before been charged upon me, of swinging a beetle to knock down a fly."

Truth always agrees with itself. And the fairest of all possible tests of the value of such a record is applied in its minute comparison with facts otherwise well known, which stand in a relation so close to it as to demonstrate its verity or its inexactness, through its conformity or its nonconformity with them. To such a test I now propose to subject the various statements above made.

1. To begin with the covenant. I make no objection to that as being an instrument probable for such use at that time;[18] but I must question the plausibility of a small portion of its phraseology. The clause "whofe names are underwritten," has no counterpart in any authentic early document of the sort which I have ever seen, and appears to have a somewhat later flavor.[19] The act of covenanting in those days evidently emphasized itself as a deed of public engagement and avowal, rather than of more private mutual written contract. This may best be shown by placing side by side the earliest three formulæ of the sort with which I am acquainted — thus:

1593.[20]	1606.[21]	1616.[22]
DEPOSITION OF DANIEL BUCK.	THE MAYFLOWER CHURCH.	MR. JACOB'S CHURCH.
Being afked what vowe or promife hee made when hee came firft to yʳ Societie, hee aunfwereth & fayth yᵗ he made yˢ *Proteftation*, viz.: That hee wold walke with yᵉ reſt of ym ſo longe as they did walke in yᵉ way of yᵉ Lorde, & as farr as might bee warranted by yᵉ Word of God.	As yᵉ Lords free people, joyned them felves (by a covenant of the Lord) into a Church Eftate in yᵉ felowfhip of yᵉ gofpell: *To walke in all his wayes, made known, or to be made known unto them, according to their beft endeauours, whatfoeuer it fhould coft them, the Lord affifting them.*	*Standing together, they joined hands,* and folemnly covenanted with each other, in the prefence of Almighty God: *To walk together in all Gods wayes and ordinances, according as he had already revealed, or fhould further make them known to them.*

---

[17] *Golden Rule*, 4 Dec. 1880.
[18] The New York *Independent*, in July, 1880, did thus object. In noticing this document as then found in the columns of *Zion's Advocate*, it said:

So far as our reading goes, church covenants were not in use during that period. They are a rather more modern invention, coming into use during the next age.

But this overlooks the fact, abundantly evidenced, that the church afterwards officered by Johnson and Ainsworth was using such a covenant in 1593, and that Neal gives, in almost the same words, the covenant by which, in 1616, Henry Jacob's church in London was confederate.

[19] The earliest near approach to this form of words which I recall, is in the covenant of the church in Bury St. Edmunds, 21 Dec. 1649 [Browne, *Hist. Congm. in Norfolk and Suffolk*, etc. 395]: "Wee whofe names are here fubfcribed, etc."

We find the exact phrafeology in the covenant of the church of which Doddridge was afterwards paftor, at Northampton, at some date apparently a few years prior to 1695 [Coleman, *Memorials Independent Chh's Northamptonshire*, etc. p. 11]: "We, this church of Chrift, *whofe names are underwritten*, etc.

[20] *Ha leinu MSS.* 7042, p. 399.
[21] Bradford, *Hist. Plim. Plant.* 9.
[22] Neal, *Hist. Puritans* (ed. 1837), i: 462.

The phrase "baptized belieuers," also, although common fifty years later, seems to be of doubtful authenticity in the sixteenth century in the North of England. The five signatures here declared to be attached to the covenant, I will at present criticise no further than to suggest that we shall by and by find reason to question the accuracy of the Christian names of two of them, and that there is the best of evidence that other two at this time represented lads respectively of eight and sixteen years of age — most unlikely to be so set forward and honored.

2. The second entry suggests a few inaccuracies, in little things, running through the extracts, which may be noted together here:

(1.) It is stated that the "moon ſhone bright" *at midnight of 20 November, 1598.* But Robert Watson's *New Almanacke, etc. for this preſent yeare 1598,*[23] states that the full moon for November of that year, was "on the iiid daye, iii minutes after two of ye clocke in ye morning;" which would make the twentieth day to be two days after the *new* moon — so that the amount of moonlight available at midnight of that date, could hardly have aided much in the dipping even of William Bradford.

(2.) On the other hand, it is further set down that, at the baptism of John Smyth, 24 March, 1606, although it was "faire aboue-head," it was so dark at midnight that they could not see without torches. Of course, if fair overhead, the moon, if there were any, must have had entire opportunity to shine. But I have the authority of Prof. Pickering of the Harvard College Observatory,[24] for stating that the moon came to the full at the meridian of Greenwich in the afternoon of 23 March, 1606; so that this baptism took place *the night after the full moon;* when, with an unobscured sky, it could not have been as dark as is here represented.

(3.) It is stated that, on 12 February, 1604, John Smyth came inquiring for the "views" of these people, and debated nearly all night upon them. But 12 February, 1604, was *Sunday;* a most unlikely day for one who was, and who — according to the statement herein made — remained for more than two years longer, vicar of Gainsborough, to have been thus engaged fifteen or twenty miles away from his own Church Service.

(4.) The term "Pædobaptiſtry" — under date of 7 May, 1604 — seems a questionable one for that time, and has much more the savor of one or two generations later.

---

[23] *New Almanacke and Prognoſtication for this preſent yeare,* etc. B. M. [P P. 2465.] *sub dato.*

[24] "By Newcomb's *Tables of Solar Eclipses,* I infer that the moon was full March 23, 1606, in the afternoon, on the meridian of Greenwich." Edward C. Pickering, *MS. note.*

(5.) It is very unlikely that so impulsive and rapid a man as we have already seen John Smyth to be, if he embraced "yͤ fayth in yͤ true Chriſtian & Apoſtolic baptiſme" as early as 7 May, 1604, should have waited until the last day of 1606 [25] — two years, ten months and seventeen days — before being rebaptized.

(6.) It is noted that William Bradford "wiſhed to ſpeake at Crowle Croſſe" on 16 February, 1607, and that this was the "next *Tueſday*" after 10 February. But 16 February, 1607, was *Monday*.

(7.) It is declared that John Norcott was "choſe as yͤ Elder of yͤ Church" on [4 April, 1609] the very day of his admission to that church, and *precisely eleven months and twenty days before he was baptized!* This follows from the fact that by Old Style — which was in universal use in England until 2 September, 1752 [26] (or more than one hundred and forty years after the events here set down) — the 24th of March was the last day of the year; which would make 4 April, 1609, the eleventh, and 24 March, 1609, the three hundred and sixty-fifth day of the same year. Improbable as such church membership and preferment of an unbaptized man must be, in itself, the more in the case of a small church which, if these records are to be taken in evidence, already had *eight* elders; that unlikelihood is increased by the fact, which will be made evident further on, that John Norcott could not have been born for nearly a quarter of a century after this date.

(8.) The entry of 4 April, 1609, purports to be certified by the signatures of four Elders. If this be authentic, the predilection of this church for youthful officers seems something wonderful; inasmuch as, at this date, Bradford was scarcely nineteen, Winslow not six months over thirteen, and Prince — who was born in 1600 or 1601 — between eight and nine years of age!

(9.) The sudden and unannounced appearance in the summer of 1620 of Enoch Clapham [*he* wrote his name Henoche] upon the scene, rises very nearly to the acme of absurdity. Nearly thirty years before ordained a minister of the Established Church by Bishop Wickham, after preaching some years in Lancashire, he associated with the Separatists and went to Holland, thence to Scotland, then to Holland again, then back to Scotland, and once more to the Netherlands; whence, leaving the Separation and returning to England, he preached in Southwark nine sermons on Tares, out of which he made a book. In the time of the great plague he discoursed unacceptably, and was committed

---

[25] It must be remembered that these dates, if genuine, are in Old Style, so that the year began on 25 March; and 24 March, 1606, would be ten months and seventeen days after, instead of one month and thirteen days before, 7 May, 1606, as, by New Style, it would be.

[26] The day after Wednesday 2 September, being called Thursday 14 September, by *Statute* 24, *Geo. II. c. 23.*

to the Gate-house at Westminster by the Archbishop of Canterbury. Down to 1609 — that is, during the first eighteen years of his ministry — he had published eleven volumes which I can trace, after which date I find none. From the general tone of these books, I do not believe it possible that he could have lived eleven years longer in silence, and I therefore presume him to have gone to his rest — he seems to have had little on earth — long before the date when he is herein named as at Crowle.[27] In any event, taking his own words in testimony, particularly some in one of his latest known works,[28] one would nearly as soon have expected to find Lyman Beecher or Thomas Binney joining the Mormons, as to find Clapham in his old age an Anabaptist Elder!

(10.) As to "provinces" in the autumn of 1617 "*lately* difcovered by Sir Walter Raleigh in Virginia:" not to press the point that Raleigh himself never was in North America; more than three and thirty years — or the lifetime of an entire generation — had passed since his captains Amadas and Barlow first sighted Ocracoke.

(11.) The statement [22 July, 1620] in regard to "Plimoth," with its concluding reasons why Bradford, Fuller, Tinker, Winslow and Brewster determined "not to haue no commune with Robinfon, etc.;" as Prince Henry said, is "laughter for a month, and a good jest forever!"

I now proceed to look at these pretended records a little more closely, in connection with what they have to say in regard to the more prominent of the actors therein.

3. As to *Samuel Fuller* two statements are made, viz.:

(1.) *1615, February*, that he returned "a dejected foule" from Holland;
(2.) *1619*, ———, that he sold his estate (presumably in Crowle, or its neighborhood) to "goe to Merica."

Now among the few things that we positively know about Samuel Fuller are: (1) that he lived in London before going to Holland;[29] (2) that he was in Amsterdam with Robinson's people in 1608-9;[30] (3) that he buried a child in St. Peter's, Leyden, 29 June, 1615;[31] (4) that he lived in the *Pieterfkerkhoff*

---

[27] I have taken these facts mainly from his own pen in the "Epistle to the Reader" of his *Antidoton; or a Sovereigne remedie againft Schifme and Herefie*, etc. (1600) 4°, pp. 48. [Bodleian. (H. 9. Th.)]

[28] I refer particularly to his *Errour on the Right Hand through a Prepofterous Zeale*, etc. (1608) 12°, pp. 70, [B. M. (1020. e. 9. (1.)]] in which he is tremendoufly severe upon Separatists and Anabaptists. It is fair to add that he followed this with *Errour on the Left Hand through a Frozen Securitie* (1608), 12°, [B. M. (1020. e. 9. (2.)]] in which he vividly depicts the evils which afflicted the Establishment, and indicates that he held a fairly evangelical conservative position.

[29] *Echt-boeck*, etc. B. p. 19.

[30] Lawne's *Prophane Schifme*, etc. 11, 24, 76.

[31] *Regifter van de Overledene perfonen Begraven binnen Leyden*, No. 3, p. 167.

in Leyden in July, 1615; (5) that he buried his wife Agnes in St. Peter's 3 July, 1615;[32] (6) that he was married again in Leyden 27 May, 1617;[33] (7) that he then lived near the *Mare-poort* in Leyden;[34] and (8) that he was one of the witnesses of John Goodman's marriage there, 5 October, 1619.[35]

All of which is violently incompatible with the assertions made with regard to him in these papers.

4. Of *Edward Winslow* we find four averments, viz.:

(1.) *1609, 4 April*, that he signed the Crowle record as an Elder;
(2.) *1615, February*, that he returned to Crowle, as one of the "dejected foules," from Holland;
(3.) *1619, ———*, that he sold his estate (in Crowle or neighborhood) "to goe to Merica;"
(4.) *1620, 22 July*, that, as an Elder of Crowle church, he renounced communion with Robinson and his company.

Now of Winslow we know: (1) that he was born at Droitwich, Eng. 18 Oct. 1595;[36] (2) that, by consequence, he was precisely thirteen years, five months and seventeen days old, when represented above to be signing church records as an elder; (3) that he lived in London before going to Leyden;[37] (4) that instead of returning in a dejected state from Holland in the spring of 1615 (when he would be scarce five months beyond his nineteenth year) there is no evidence that he ever was in Holland at all before 1617;[38] that at Leyden, 13 May, 1618, he married Elizabeth Barker;[39] and (5) finally, that he was in Leyden 10 June, 1620;[40] heard Mr. Robinson's farewell discourse (for the preservation of all knowledge of which we are indebted to his pen) early in July;[41] sailed from Delfs-Haven in the Speedwell 12 July;[42] and was with the Mayflower company at Southampton making ready for their voyage across the Atlantic on that very July day on which he is above misrepresented as having renounced all fellowship with them. Comment is needless.

---

[32] *Ibid.*
[33] *Echt-boeck*, etc. B. p. 64.
[34] *Ibid.*
[35] *Ibid.* p. 90.
[36] Transcript of Parish Record, *N. E. Hist. & Gen. Reg.* 1867, p. 210.
[37] *Echt-boeck*, etc. B. p. 75.
[38] He himself says [*Hypocrisie Vnmasked*, etc. p. 93]: "I living three yeares under his [Mr. Robinson's] Ministery, before we began the worke of Plantation in *New-England*." This would throw back his going to Leyden to reside, to the summer of 1617.
[39] *Echt-boeck*, etc. B. p. 75.
[40] With Fuller, Bradford and Allerton [see *Bradford*, p. 51], he signed at Leyden a letter of date 1-10 June, 1620, to Carver and Cushman in London.
[41] He reports this from memory [*Hypocrisie Vnmasked*, etc. p. 97] as if he heard it, and his language can fairly warrant no other conclusion than that he did.
[42] He says [*Ibid.* p. 90]:

And when the Ship was ready to carry us away, the Brethren that stayed having againe solemnly sought the Lord with us, and for us, and we further engaging our selves mutually as before; they, I say, that stayed at Leyden feasted us that were to goe at our Pastors house being large, where wee refreshed our selves after our teares, with singing of Psalmes, making joyfull melody in our hearts, as well as with the voice, there being many of the Congregation very expert in Musick; and indeed it was the sweetest melody that ever mine eares heard. After this they accompanyed us to *Delphs-Haven*, where wee were to imbarque, and there feasted us againe: and after prayer performed by our Pastor, where a flood of teares was poured out, they accompanyed us to the Ship, etc.

5. Of *John Carver* three things are declared, viz.:

(1.) *1609, 4 April*, that, as Elder of Crowle church, he signed its records;
(2.) *1615, February*, that he returned "dejected" from Holland;
(3.) *1619,* ———, that he sold his property in that region to "goe to Merica."

For so good, and probably great, a man, our knowledge of John Carver is singularly scanty. But we do know a few things, as follows, viz.: (1) that, to appearance — the record is not clear — he was in Leyden, and buried a child in St. Pancras, 10 July, 1609;[43] (2) that he was in Leyden at a marriage, 28 May, 1616;[44] (3) that he was at another there, 23 Mar. 1617;[45] (4) and at still another 18 August, 1618;[46] (5) that he was a deacon of Robinson's church;[47] (6) that he was sent from Leyden to London as an agent of Robinson's congregation in the autumn of 1617;[48] (7) that he was sent again on a like errand in the spring of 1620;[49] (8) that he went from Leyden to Delfs-Haven and Southampton with the company in July, 1620; (9) received a letter at Southampton from John Robinson of date 27 July, 1620;[50] and (10) was chosen Governor of one of the ships for the expedition — a choice confirmed for the whole Colony, 11 November following, in Provincetown harbor.[51] Which things could not have been true of him were the Crowle records authentic.

6. We now come to *John Norcott*, concerning whom these papers include six statements, viz.:

(1.) *1609, 24 March*, that he was baptized in the Torne by John Smyth;
(2.) *1609, 4 April*, that he was received at the Lord's Supper;
(3.) *1609, 4 April*, that he was chosen an Elder of the Church;
(4.) *1609, 4 April*, that he started with others for Holland;
(5.) *1613,* ———, that he had written a quaint but scriptural book on Baptism, which was printed in Holland;
(6.) *1614 — November* (?), that he died suddenly at Amsterdam of putrid fever, and was buried in the same grave with John Smyth.

As to these particulars there are four things only needing here to be said. (1) As will be seen by turning back,[52] John Smyth had been in Amsterdam two or three years at the time when he is above made to have been at Epworth performing this baptism; (2) he had certainly been dead and buried in Am-

---

[43] *Register van de Overledene personen*, etc. No. 3, p. 10. The handwriting is very blind, and the name may be John something else, but Baron Elsevier, archivist of Leyden, inclines to read it *Carver*. A like record occurs (*Reg.* No. 4, p. 8) under date of 11 Nov. 1617.
[44] *Echt-boeck*, etc. B. p. 51.
[45] *Ibid.* p. 60.
[46] *Ibid.* p. 77.
[47] *Bradford*, p. 32.
[48] *Ibid.* pp. 30–32.
[49] *Ibid.* p. 43.
[50] *Ibid.* p. 63.
[51] *Ibid.* pp. 68, 90.
[52] p. 2 of this pamphlet.

sterdam more than two years, when he is here represented as dying and sharing John Norcott's interment there;[53] while (3) Ivimey[54] states that the John Norcott, who wrote that *Baptism Discovered*, etc. which, beyond question,[55] must be the book referred to, as "quaint, but according to ye Bible," having "probably shortened his days by his excessive labours," after a ministry that "was but short," died "in middle life," 24 March, 1675-6, pastor of the church in Gravel-lane, Wapping. But if he died "in middle life," he could not have been over forty-five years of age; and if he were five and forty at his death in 1676, he must have been born not earlier than 1630 — or one and twenty years after the first, and sixteen years after the last mention of his name in these Crowle "records." And, finally (4), the book which is here represented to have been printed in Holland in or about 1613, appears, in reality, to have been first put to press about *fifty-seven years later* in *England.*[56]

7. We next reach *John Morton*, or, as he himself wrote his name, *John Murton*, of whom nine declarations are made, to wit, that:

(1.) *1599, 4 January*, he signed the original church covenant as an Elder;
(2.) *1604, 12 February*, as a Crowle Elder he debated with John Smyth;
(3.) *1606, 24 March*, he baptized John Smyth in the Don;
(4.) *1609, 30 March*, he met the church in consultation about emigration;
(5.) *1609, 4 April*, he started with Smyth and others for Holland;
(6.) *1615, February*, he came back among the "dejected;"
(7.) *1615, 16 March*, he went to Collingham, etc. to order things;
(8.) *1617, 10 November*, he came back from Chichester;
(9.) *1617, ———*, he fell sick, died, and was buried at Butterwick.

---

[53] *Ibid.* p. 38.
[54] iii: 296, 298.
[55] "Beyond question" — because there is neither trace of any other John Norcott, nor of any other book on Baptism by any kind of a Norcott: because the phrase "quaint but according to ye Bible" might very fairly be applied (by a Baptist critic) to the book in its original form: and because the author dedicates it "To his truly beloved *Friends and Brethren in and about Wapping*," etc., thus identifying the Wapping pastor as its author. Mr. Spurgeon — who can hardly be congratulated on special eminence as an antiquary (*non omnia possumus omnes*) — published a new edition of it, "corrected and somewhat altered," in 1878, in the preface to which he said [p. vi]:

The little book which is here presented to you, almost in its ancient form, was first printed in Holland more than 200 years ago, by a servant of the Lord who was in exile for the faith.

If Mr. Spurgeon had taken the trouble to examine the earliest edition now accessible in the British Museum — which is the fifth — [4326. aa.] he would have found in it an "Epistle Dedicatory" to the third edition, signed by William Kiffin and R. C. [Richard Claridge], which says:

What Approbation this Piece hath found may appear from hence; that *since the First Edition of it here in England*, it hath been *Reprinted* in Holland, was also lately translated into Welsh; and now growing scarce and much asked for, the Bookseller hath been Advised to give it another Impression.

[56] Watt does not mention the book. The Dr. Williams Library has the third edition, of date 1694, the earliest which I have met with. We have then [see last note] these four data: (1) The *third* edition in 1694; (2) The *second* (English) published in Holland; (3) the *first*, published in England while its author was pastor at Wapping. (4) As he says in his dedication: "Our Sun is going down, eternity is upon us," etc., it is fairly to be presumed that this first edition was published not long before his death in March, 1676: from all which its date cannot reasonably be put earlier than 1670, where I place it [App. No. 276].

[76]

Put by the side of the above dates and declarations the following facts, viz.: (1) that John Murton was born in 1582 or 1583,[57] and was consequently little if any more than twenty-one years of age when he is represented as being so effective in debate as an Elder with an old hand like Smyth; (2) that he lived in Gainsborough (or Queensborough[58]) before going to Amsterdam; (3) that he was in Amsterdam 23 August, 1608, because he, on that date, announced to the magistrates of that city his intention, being 25 years of age, to marry Jane Hodgkin of Worksop, who was 23;[59] (4) that, in the room of his baptizing Smyth in the Don in 1606, at some time in 1608 Smyth rebaptized *him* at Amsterdam;[60] (5) that so far from coming among the "poor dear dejected" back to Crowle in February, 1615, he had two or three years before returned, in good courage, to England and founded a Baptist church in London at Newgate;[61] and (6) that instead of dying, and laying his "wēry bones," in "yᵉ front of yᵉ meeting door" at Butterwick in 1617, he was alive and vigorous in his London pastorate as late as 13 November, 1626.[62]

8. We have next eleven entries touching *William Bradford*, thus:

(1.) *1598, 20 November*, he was baptized in the Torne;
(2.) *1599, 4 January*, was an Elder of Crowle church;
(3.) *1607, 10 February*, announced to "holde fourth" at Crowle Crosse;
(4.) *1607, 16 February*, tried it, but the parson and his dog prevented;
(5.) *1609, 30 March*, met with the church about emigrating;
(6.) *1609, 4 April*, started after liberty of conscience in an open boat;
(7.) *1609, 4 April*, signed record as Elder stating that fact;
(8.) *1615, February*, came back from Holland among the "deare dejected;"
(9.) *1615, 16 March*, started for Collingham, etc. to set things to rights;
(10.) *1619, ———*, sold his property in Crowle, or thereabouts, to "goe to Merika;"
(11.) *1620, 22 July*, renounced communion with Robinson and his "party."

Compare with the above the following facts, viz.: (1) we have the evidence of the Austerfield Parish Records, remaining in beautiful parchment, that William Bradford was baptized 19 March, 1589–90[63]—he would, consequently, have been only *eight years, eight months and one day* old when he is said to have been immersed as an adult; (2) he would have been only *nine years, nine months and sixteen days* old, when he is here represented to be signing the covenant as an

---

[57] Amsterdam *Puy-boeck*, 1606–12. s. d. 23 Aug. 1608.
[58] The record says *Queynsborch*, which might stand for either. The Dutch scribes spelled as they liked, *e.g.* Blossom is once *Blase*, and Goodman *Coedmoer*/
[59] *Ibid.*
[60] See pp. 10, 30, 32, *ante.*

[61] See p. 42, *ante*. See also *Truths Victory*, etc. (1645) p. 19.
[62] *Letter of C. C. Aresto*, Evans, ii: 25, 33.
[63] I cite the original. A transcript may also be found in Hunter, *Collections concerning Scrooby Church*, etc. (1854) p. 198.

[77]

Elder of the church; (3) he would have been but *sixteen years, ten months and twenty-six days* old on that memorable day of the encounter with the parson and "the bull-dogge;" (4) his own history shews [64] that having lived in Amsterdam "aboute a year," as early as in February, 1609, he was making arrangements, which were perfected by the first of May of that year, to remove to Leyden; [65] (5) instead of coming back "dejected" from Amsterdam to Crowle in February, 1615, he was assisting Samuel Lee to citizenship in Leyden on 19 October of that year; [66] instead of selling property in Crowle and its neighborhood preparing to "goe to Merika" in 1619, he sold in Leyden 19 April of that year a house on the north side of the *Achtergracht*,[67] and, 7 June following, aided William Ring to become a citizen there; [68] and in 1620, shared in the departure of the Pilgrim fathers from Delfs-Haven, and all their fortunes at Southampton, Dartmouth and Plymouth, with their subsequent Mayflower voyage — there being no evidence that he ever set foot in England from the day of his first leaving it for Amsterdam, till, in July, 1620, he disembarked from the Speedwell in Southampton Water.

9. Turn we now to *William Brewster*, as to whom there are the eight following assertions, viz.:

(1.) *1599, 4 January*, that he was an Elder of Crowle Church;
(2.) *1603, 3 November*, that he agreed with a sea-captain to remove 72 of the Crowle Company from Boston to Amsterdam;
(3.) *1603, November*, that by treachery he was lodged in prison, and lay a month in Lincoln jail;
(4.) *1606, 24 March*, that he offered prayer at the midnight baptism of Smyth in the Don;
(5.) *1609, 30 March*, that he met to consult with the church about emigration;
(6.) *1615, February*, that, as one of the "deare dejected," he returned from Hoiland;
(7.) *1619, ———*, that, with others, he sold his estate in or near Crowle; and
(8.) *1620, 22 July*, that he joined with Bradford, Clapham, Fuller, Winslow and Tinker in renouncing communion with Robinson.

It will be quite sufficient to set the memory of William Brewster right concerning these asseverations, if we note: (1) that, from 1 April, 1594, for many years he filled the place at Scrooby as agent of the Archbishop of York which his father had filled before him, and was Postmaster there; [69] and that he continued thus in Government employ until 30 September, 1607 [70] — a fact which,

---

[64] *Hist. Plim. Plant.* etc. 16.
[65] *Gerechts Dag-boeck* (Leyden), (G.) p. 34.
[66] *Poorter-boeck* (Leyden), *begonst in den Jare 1603, ende Ge-eijn-dight in den Jare 1635*, (F.) p. 91.
[67] *Op Dragts-boecken-van huisen* (V.V.) p. 135.
[68] *Poorter-boeck*, etc. (F.) p. 120.
[69] P. R. O. *Dom. Eliz.* vol. 233, no. 48.
[70] Hunter, *Collections*, etc. 68.

in those jealous days, must have been irreconcilable with the first four of them; (2) that, with Bradford and the others, he had been in Amsterdam a twelvemonth, and was just about removing with them to Leyden, at the date of the fifth;[71] that instead of returning to England in 1615, he was chosen by John Robinson's church in Leyden "an affiftant unto him in ye place of an Elder;"[72] that in 1617, 1618 and 1619 he was publishing books, Latin and English, in Leyden;[73] that in 1619 he was sent to London as an agent in the negotiations about the removal to New England;[74] and that, in 1620, instead of renouncing communion with Robinson and his company, he led off in the emigration to New Plymouth in a harmony of both doctrinal and practical feeling, desire, and design, with his beloved and honored pastor which was so perfect, that it is hard to say whether the Crowle falsehood which declares the contrary, excels in its unveracity or its impudence.[75]

10. I have reserved inquiry as to *John Smyth* until the last needing special investigation as to the tone of these "records" with regard to them, partly because, in some aspects, he was the most noteworthy of the company; but mainly because his case has one peculiarity. It can scarcely be called violently probable, yet the human mind is able to conceive it possible, that there should have been contemporaneously living during the first quarter of the seventeenth century, in England and thereabouts, two Samuel Fullers, and two Edward Winslows, and two John Carvers (there surely were not two John Norcotts), and two John Murtons, and two William Bradfords, and two William Brewsters, concerning one set of whom the statements made in these Crowle papers might be facts; as, concerning the other set of whom, the statements which I have accumulated above from various authentic sources surely were facts; so that an enthusiastic and inappeasable champion of those "records" might still insist that, granting the truth of all which I claim to be true, all which those documents allege may still be also true — of other men of the same names. Waiving then, for the present, all inference from what has gone before, it will be agreed on all hands as inconceivable that there can have been two John Smyths, *both vicar of Gainsborough, in and about 1600.* This name, then, furnishes the opportunity for a crucial test, which shall now be applied. Nine distinct declarations are made concerning him. Thus:

---

[71] Vide Bradford's *Hist. Plym. Plant.* 16; Dialogue, etc. *Young,* 466.

[72] *Bradford,* p. 17.

[73] See the titles of three such volumes in Latin and seven in English, under these three years, in the Appendix of *Congregationalism as Seen,* etc. Besides these I have surely traced other two in Latin, and one in English.

[74] *Bradford,* p. 30.

[75] This lies on the face of Bradford's whole account of the removal, with the arrangements that led to, and the correspondence which followed, it.

(1.) *1604, 12 February.* "John Smith, Vicar of Gainſborough," inquired and debated.
(2.) *1604, 7 May.* He acknowledged his conversion to Anti-pædobaptistry, proposed to be rebaptized, discoursed sweetly, and announced his intention to resign his vicarage.
(3.) *1606, 24 March.* After subsequently waiting a time, for him, most extraordinary [two years, ten months and seventeen days] he, "John Smith, Vicar of Gainſborough," was baptized in the Don, having "made a good confeſſion."
(4.) *1607, 10 February.* He is declared to have — another extraordinary thing for him — been holding "silent meetings."
(5.) *1609, 30 March.* He — "late Vicar of Gainſborough " — shared in the church debate about emigrating to Holland.
(6.) *1609, 4 April.* He administered the sacrament in an "apple-chamber," and received John Norcott to the church.
(7.) *1609, 4 April.* On the same day — it was Tuesday — he started with John Norcott and others down the Trent in an open boat, bound for Hull, Holland, and liberty of conscience.
(8.) *1609, 24 March.* He and Norcott seem to have come back together from the Low Countries, in order that he might baptize that mythical young man — who had been already, in his unbaptized state, a church member, and an Elder, for eleven months and twenty days — in the Torne ; — doubtless better than all Dutch waters in which to wash and be clean.
(9.) *1614, December.* The painful news of his decease — and that of the mythical young man — both dying suddenly of *putrid fever*, and sharing one grave, reaches the bereaved remnant at Crowle.

To take the last first, we have already seen that the burial records of the *Nieuwe Kerk* at Amsterdam contain the proof that Smyth was interred there *1 September, 1612*, or a little more than *two years previous to the date here assigned;* and that he died of *a consumption*, having been sick *seven weeks*.[76] We have also already seen that the third, fourth, fifth, sixth and seventh of these statements cannot be true, because Smyth went to Amsterdam with his Gainsborough company in October or November, 1606,[77] and there is no evidence that he ever revisited England. As to the first, second, and eighth, all which can be needful to destroy any possible remnant of probability which in any mind may still attach to them, will be to recall attention to the fact that Smyth never accepted the Baptist theory of believers' baptism until 1609 ;[78] and that in the very month in which he is here represented to have been baptizing Norcott in the Torne in the North of England, having been excommunicated from the church he had formed at the date of his se-baptism in Amsterdam, he was vainly asking a Mennonite church in that city to receive him, while Murton, Helwys, Pygott and Seamer were remonstrating against such reception ;[79] with some further proof of the uniform Pædobaptist tenor of his

---

[76] See pp. 37 and 38, and notes 167, 166, 165, *ante*.
[77] p. 2 and note 13, *ante*.
[78] See p. 9, *ante*.
[79] See pp. 36 and 37, *ante*.

books down to his *Character of the Beaſt*, printed also in 1609. Let us glance at these.

(1.) *Principles and Inferences*, etc. [1607]. This of course was sent forth three years after these "records" assure us that its author had renounced "Pædobaptiſtry," and one year after they say he had been rebaptized. Yet among these 203 Principles or Inferences, there is not the slightest reference to the mode or subjects of Baptism — a thing incredible were the author already a convert to the notion that that subject requires to be made the corner stone of churches.

(2.) *The Diferences of the Churches of the Separation*, etc. [summer of 1608].[80] Here, again, although the book was expressly written to "clear further" the truth, he never once alludes to Baptism as a subject of doubt, difficulty, or debate — showing that his opinions on that subject still remained at one with those then common among the Separatists.

(3.) *Paralleles, Censures, Obſervations*, etc. [I think late in 1608, although dated 1609]. Here, down almost to the very epoch of his re-baptism by se-baptism, we find him:

(*a*) identifying himself still with "the Browniſts," whose doctrine he declares to be "the vndoubted truth of God;"[81]

(*b*) denouncing Anabaptists, in common with "Papists" and "Arrians," etc. as "heretiques;"[82]

(*c*) objecting against the baptism of the Church of England, not because of any defect in manner, or error as to its subjects, but simply because that church is "not the true body of 'Chriſt, the true Church of God, therefore all the holy things are profaned when they are ther adminiſtred;"[83]

(*d*) and, finally, by distinctly saying that *all which he asks as to reform on the subject of baptism in the Church of England,* is that infant baptism "be adminiſtred ſimply, as Chriſt teacheth: without Godfathers, the croſſe, queſtions to infants, etc."[84]

This must necessarily be conclusive that down to a period nearly five years later than the date of his alleged full conversion to immersionist views — saying nothing of dipping, which he never accepted — Smyth had not gotten so far as that fundamental tenet of the Baptists, of baptism for adult believers alone. No Baptist out of a lunatic asylum could have written the sentence last quoted above!

---

[80] See p. 8, and note 42, *ante*.
[81] pp. 109, 119, 135.
[82] See p. 4, note 27, *ante*.
[83] pp. 117, 139, 140.
[84] p. 79.

I find in these alleged records of this ancient Baptist church, eighty distinct statements, as to twenty different individuals. I have now minutely, and as I trust candidly, examined from them two assertions as to Samuel Fuller, four as to Edward Winslow, three as to John Carver, six as to John Norcott, nine as to John Murton, eleven as to William Bradford, eight as to William Brewster, and nine as to John Smyth — fifty-two in all; and have proved *every one of them* to be, if not impossible, at least improbable with an intensity in most cases equivalent to moral incredibility. I have pointed out, further, eleven cases of palpable disagreement with well established facts. As to Henoch Clapham and Thomas Prence I have shown further unlikelihoods. Thomas Petch I never heard of before, and, considering that the only thing which he is said to have done, is, to have brought from Holland the misstatement that a man who had died of a lingering consumption two years before, was then just suddenly deceased of putrid fever, I never care to hear of him again. This disposes of eleven of the twenty persons, and of six and sixty of the eighty "facts" — leaving nine unimportant men and fourteen unessential assertions unexamined as yet; concerning whom, and which, more directly.

The candid reader who bears in mind the two facts: (1) that in the case of the eight prominent persons whose relation to this record has been considered, every one of the two and fifty averments made in regard to them has been shown to be unfounded; and (2) that in the case of John Smyth, "vicar of Gainsborough," well-meant mistake was impossible, and no conclusion other than that of an attempt at the deliberate perversion of history remains credible; will now be prepared to join me in the conclusion that these newly-discovered leaves out of an old oaken chest are — *falsum in uno, falsum in omnibus* — all together, an unblushing forgery; undertaken by some excessively ill-informed person, and carried out in a singularly stupid and bungling manner. A few words further on that subject.

And here let me say, at once, that I acquit the Rev. Mr. Stutterd of all complicity with such an attempt, and all suspicion of it. He impressed me as an honest and good man, much more likely, in his comparatively uncultured simplicity in regard to such subjects, to be imposed upon, than to undertake imposition upon others. In answer to my inquiries at the time he told me that the "original records" which he copied, seemed written neither on paper nor parchment, but on something reminding him of plantain leaf; that the ink now and then was very faded; and that the leaves were much decayed and eaten by small red insects discernible under a magnifier; so that in parts it was only with the greatest difficulty that the contents could be made out at all. Anxious to get possession of all the facts, I addressed him a note on my return to

London, which, with his reply, I append — for convenience placing my questions and his answers in parallel.

Grand Hotel, London, 9 May, 1881.

Rev. Jabez Stutterd,

Dear Sir: Two or three inquiries have suggested themselves to me, which I ought to have proposed to you, in reference to the very interesting records of your church, when I saw you the other day: but, as they escaped me at that time, I venture to send them now, and ask you to be so good as to reply to them in the enclosed envelope. I will be glad to know:

1. As nearly as possible, when, by whom, and in what place, were these leaves of the old record discovered?

2. Was any public announcement — so far as you know — of that discovery made *at the time*?

3. Of whom did you receive them for the purpose of copying them; and to whom, and when, did you return them after you had copied them?

4. Did you copy *all* of that record which referred to matters of public interest, of the general character of those which you did copy?

5. When were you first made acquainted with the fact that the originals are since lost; and from whom did you learn it?

6. Do you think any thorough and sufficient

Crowle, Lincolnshire,
Via Doncaster,
12 May, 1881.

My dear Sir,

Yours of yesterday arrived, but found me from home.

1. The old records were discovered at Butterwick in a chest of an old Baptist family, by the Rev. Smith Watson many years ago. In 1866 I first saw them at Revd. Smith Watson's, and copied the 7 or 8 leaves, moth-eaten and decayed as they were. Some two or three weeks I had them.

2. No public announcement was made at the time. At length by the wish and desire of the members and deacons of the Church, and not on my own responsibility, a portion of it was sent to our own Magazine for preservation.

3. I received them of Revd. Smith Watson. And when copied they were returned to his care again, after being carefully copied in the presence of some of our Brethren. This was in 1866.

4. I copied all I possibly could which related to matters of interest — from the damp and moth-eaten records.

5. About four years ago, when preaching at Butterwick, we wanted to see them, and refer to them again, but we could not find them anywhere. When Smith Watson died his goods and chattels were divided amongst his friends, who all say they have not seen anything of them [*i. e.* the records]. These particulars I have had over and over again from his relatives.

6. A thorough and severe search has been

search has been made to recover the lost manuscript; and is it to your mind perfectly clear that it is now of no use to undertake at Epworth, or Butterwick, or elsewhere, any further inquiry for the missing records?

7. Should you imagine there could be the slightest probability that, in copying the manuscript, in its confessedly imperfect and illegible state, you mistook and miscopied names; so that, for the names of William Bradford, John Carver, Edward Winslow, Samuel Fuller, and John Smyth — for example — as given in your copy, other names ought to be substituted, in order *exactly* to render the original?

8. Is there the slightest doubt in your mind that the fragment which you copied was a *genuine portion of the original records of your church?* Or do you conceive it as barely *possible* that some mischievous or designing person could have prepared such an (apparently) ancient manuscript, in the view and intent to deceive you, and others, into the belief that it was what it really was not?

You will, my dear sir, much add to the obligations under which I already am to your kind courtesy, if you will reply to the above.

I am, faithfully, yours,
HENRY M. DEXTER.
Rev. Mr. Stutterd.

made in Epworth, East and West Butterwick, in Ashby, Winterton and Hasey and other places, to recover the lost portions of the record. For the present, though, we keep making inquiries. And to my mind it seems clear that they are lost irrecoverably, but some of our friends think they may turn up, some day.

7. The greatest care was taken in copying the manuscript, for then it was falling fast into a state of decay. Possibly there might be a name copied wrong, but I am not aware such is the case. We are all imperfect in this imperfect world.

8. I have no doubt whatever on my mind but what was copied was a genuine portion of the original records. My Brethren here think the same. I cannot entertain the opinion that some mischievous or ill-designing person could prepare such a Document for the sake of deceiving.

Dear Sir, I have replied with pleasure to your enquiries,
And believe me,
Yours truly,
JABEZ STUTTERD.

The well informed student of New England history who has closely examined the pretended extracts printed near the beginning of this chapter, will, long since, no doubt, have reached the conclusion that, if left to stand solely on their own probability — as Mr. Stutterd's letter above clearly shows they must be — they cannot possibly be assigned to a date earlier than 1856 — while probably written some years later. The evidence of this I will now produce, by asking the reader to examine with minutest care the passages which I now place side by side.

Things have come to fuch a paffe . . . . . . it has been refolved . . . that for the fake of peace we fhall leaue this our dear

Seeing them felves thus molefted, and that ther was no hope of their continuance ther, by a joynte confente they refolued to goe into native countrye & retire to Holland, wher, we heare, there is freedome of religion for all men. Wee fhall haue to learne a newe language, and get our liuings we know not how. It is a dear place & fubject to ye mifferies of warre : is thought by many of ye brethren, an adventure almoft defperate, a cafe intolerable, & a mifferie worfe then death. Efpetially feeing our brethren are not acquainted with trads nor traffique (by which Hollanders fubfifte) but wee are ufed to plain countrie life and farming.

Wee have refolued to pray vnceafinglie : our chiefe difficultie is wee cannot ftay, yet wee are not fuffered to goe ; for ye Ports & Hauens are fhut againft us, fo wee muft looke for fecrete meanes of conveyance, fee ye failers, & pay high rates for our paffage.

ye Low-Countries, wher they heard was freedome of Religion for all men . . . . they muft learne a new language, and get their liuings they knew not how ; it being a dear place & fubjecte to ye mifferies of warr, it was by many thought an adventure almoft defperate, a cafe intolerable & a mifferie worfe then death. Efpetially feeing they were not acquainted with trads nor traffique (by which yt countrie doth fubfifte) but had only been ufed to a plaine countrie life & ye innocente trade of hufbandrey. . . . .

Though they could not ftay, yet were yy not fuffered to goe, but ye ports & hauens were fhut againft them, fo as they were faine to feeke fecrete means of conveance, & to bribe & fee ye mariners, & giue exterordinarie rates for their paffages.

Any scholar familiar with such matters will see, and will say, at once, that the person who wrote one of the above statements must have had the other not merely in memory, but actually under his eye, while writing. But that in the second column was written by William Bradford in the year 1630[85] in the little settlement of New Plymouth on this side of the sea ; remained in manuscript — a part of the time in the custody of Thomas Prince in the steeple of the Old South Church — until it was purloined, carried to England and in some inexplicable way deposited in the Fulham library ; whence it was first printed in 1856 by the Massachusetts Historical Society, and where (it is charitable to suppose through the Bishop of London's ignorance that he is the keeper of stolen goods) it still remains. It is safe to say that Bradford did not copy from the Crowle "records ; " therefore the fabricator of those "records" which are printed in the first column copied from Bradford. And, as the forger could never have seen the manuscript, he copied from the printed version. He could not, therefore, have written earlier than 1856, and as it would naturally take some time for such a volume to work its way up to the North of England, he probably manufactured these " records " not very long before they were "discovered" in 1866 ; having been by him placed in the "old oaken chest" judiciously and conveniently to that end.

Following this clew we strike at once upon further probable revelations. There can hardly be reasonable doubt that the whole story of the thwarted Crowle and Epworth endeavor to flee to Holland by way of Boston in 1603,

---

[85] See Bradford's own statement, *Hist. Plym. Plant.* | etc. 6. For the extracts see pp. 10, 11 and 12.

[85]

was suggested by Bradford's account of the like attempt of the Scrooby men in 1608;[86] nor that it was, in the main, as to its language, largely suggested therefrom. For example, mark the following:

The Crowle Forgery. (1603.)

A sea-captaine who agreed to take us from Boston in this county to Amsterdam ... Wee arrived before yᵉ captaine, & had a wearie time waiting ... The vessel appeared at night ... The ship was borded by serchers & other officers, with whom our Captain was in league. In yᵉ deade of yᵉ night wee were turned out into open boats, & searched & ransaked by yᵉ officials — women as wel as men. When they had taken all our money, bookes & goods from us, they carried us before yᵉ magestrates, who ordered us off to prison, where we lay for a month ... The monthe after the greater number of us 72. were released; but Mr. Brewster & seaven others were detained & conveyed to Lincoln goale.

Bradford's History. (1608.)

At Boston in Lincolin-shire ... made agreement with the maister, etc. ... After long waiting ... he came at length & tooke them in, in yᵉ night. But when he had them & their goods abord, he betrayed them, haveing before hand complotted with yᵉ serchers & other officers so to doe; who tooke them, and put them into open boats, & ther rifled & ransaked them, searching them to their shirts for money, yea even yᵉ women furder then became modestie ... Stripte of their money, books and much other goods, they were presented to yᵉ magestrates ... and so they were comited to ward ... After a months imprisonment, yᵉ greatest parte were dismiste & sent to yᵉ places from whence they came, but 7. of yᵉ principall [foot-note, "Elder Brewster was one of these"] were still kept in prison, and bound over to yᵉ Assises.

We may now, perhaps, see our way to account for the nine men remaining. Of these Helwise was a natural suggestion; as he was always a true yokefellow of Murton, and the change of his Christian name from Thomas to Henry was either one more blunder, or a precautionary measure against over-exactness. Robert Carver appears to have been prompted in the same way, as brother of John. Edward Fuller, John Oldham, Thomas Tinker and John Turner were taken bodily from the lists of the passengers of the Mayflower, and the Anne and Little James.[87] John [James] Rayner appears to have been one of Robinson's men, and probably one of Brewster's printers.[88] John Rowe and Eli Kelsey remain. But there was a John Rowe — son of John — who was a well-known man in those days;[89] and Taylor[90] says that in 1661 there was an Anabaptist named John Kelsay in Lincolnshire, from whom — giving him another Bible Christian name — this laboring romancer could complete the roll of his *dramatis personæ*.

---

[86] *Ibid.* p. 12.
[87] *Bradford*, pp. 449, 453, 454; *Young*, 352.
[88] "Il fut imprimeur probablement avec William Brewster," etc. *MS. of M. le Baron W. J. C. Rammelman Elsevier.*
[89] Palmer's *Calamy*, i: 180.
[90] *Gen. Bap.* i: 193.

This inquiry may here be concluded. Perhaps it ought to be concluded with an apology for having occupied so much space in the examination of such unmitigated rubbish. A more despicably fraudulent endeavor to pollute the sources of history, than these alleged ancient Crowle Church records, surely does not stain the annals of English literature. Were it not that the ill effects of such deception sadden all aspects of such a case, this would be positively ludicrous for the stupendousness of its stupidity; for the absurdities growing out of its inacquaintance with so simple a fact of the past as the difference between Old Style and New; for its never-mending failure to hit any nail upon the head. If the man had thrown a font of types into the air, they could not have fallen down into feebler fables. The doctrine of the calculation of chances, if he had left it unmeddled with, must surely have somewhere yielded him at least one little single solitary fact amid his howling wilderness of lies.

As it is, one may write the epitaph of these "records" fitly in "the wordes of the Preacher, the fonne of Dauid king in Jerufalem"—injecting the reiterated noun thereof with the fulness of that classic sense of mendacity, in which Cicero in his Tusculan Questions employed it:

Vanitas Vanitatum: Vanitas Vanitatum: Et omnia Vanitas.

Collections toward a Bibliography of the First two Generations of the Baptist Controversy in England.

[The only explanation which seems to be needed here is that, in arranging books by their dates, in every case where possible I have followed Thomason's endorsement on the title-pages; printing, when they have been indicated by him, the month and day, in fine type under the year. In doing thus I have sometimes been compelled to disregard the year as set forth on the title-page.' *E. g.* No. 8 bears the printed date of 1641, but, as I have shown [note 51, p. 48 ante], it could not have been published before May, 1642. As my object herein has simply been to direct to the means of knowledge the attention of those who may doubt my statements, or who desire further to pursue lines of thought by them suggested, I have generally given only so much of a title as may accurately identify a book, and named some one library where it may be consulted. In those cases where I have not found a volume, I have sometimes indicated the source of my impression that such a book had existence. The place of publication is London, unless otherwise stated.]

1618.	A Plain and Well-grounded Treatise concerning Baptisme. [translated from the Dutch.] [*Crosby*, i: 128.]	1
1623.	[I. P.] [RESTON.]—Anabaptismes Mysterie of Iniquity Unmasked, etc. 16°, pp. xxx, 68. [contains Anabaptist letter giving grounds of separation from the Chh. of Eng. rep. by *Crosby*, i: 133–139.] B. M. [4323. a.]	2
1624.	DODD & CLEAVER.—The Patrimony of Christian Children, etc. 4°. [*Crosby*, i: 141.]	3
1641.	A Discovery of 29. Sects here in London, all of which except the first, are most Divelish and Damnable, etc. 4°, pp. 8. B. M. [E. 168. (7.)]	4
1641.	The Book of Common Prayer now used in the Church of England, vindicated from the Aspersions of all Schismatiques, Anabaptists, Brownists and Separatists; Together with a discovery of a sort of people called *Rebaptists*, lately found out in Hackney Marsh neere London, etc. 4°, pp. 8. B. M. [3475. aaa.]	5
1642. [Apr.]	[P. B.] [ARBON.]—A Discourse tending to prove the Baptisme in, or under the defection of Antichrist to be the Ordinance of Jesus Christ, as also That the Baptisme of Infants or Children, is warrantable and agreeable to the Word of God, etc. 4°, pp. viii, 32. B. M. [E. 138. (23.)]	6
[1642.] [May]	T. KILCOP.—A Short Treatise of Baptisme. Wherein is declared that only Christs disciples or beleevers are to be baptized, etc. [n. pl.] 16°, pp. iii, 13. B. M. [E. 1113. (1.)]	7
[1642.] [May]	E. BARBER.—A Small Treatise of Baptisme, or Dipping; wherein is cleerly shewed, that the Lord Christ ordained Dipping for those only that professe repentance and faith: (1) proved by Scriptures; (2) by Arguments; (3) a Parallel betwixt Circumcision and Dipping; (4) an Answere to some objections by P. B[arbon] [*i. e.* those raised in no. 6]. 4°, pp. viii, 30. B. M. [E. 143. (17.)]	8
1642. [June]	[A. R.]—A Treatise of the Vanity of Childishe Baptism; wherein the deficiency of the Baptisme of the Church of England is considered in five particulars thereof; and wherin also is proved that *Baptizing* is Dipping and Dipping *Baptizing*. 4°, pp. vi, 32. B. M. [152. (4.)]	9
1642. [4 July]	[A. R.]—The Second Part of the Vanity & Childishnes of Infants Baptisme [no. 9] wherein The grounds from Severall Scriptures usually brought for to justifie the same, are urged and answered. As also the nature of the divers Covenants made with Abraham and his seed, briefly opened and applied. 4°, pp. ii, 30. B. M. [E. 59. (5.)]	10

(87)

1642. T. WYNELL. — The Covenants Plea for Infants: or, The Covenant of Free Grace pleading the Divine   11
[5 Sept.] Right of Christian infants unto the Seale of holy Baptisme. Against the rusticke Sophistry, and
wicked Cavillations of sacrilegious Anabaptists, etc. Oxford, 4°, pp. xii, 124.
B. M. [E. 115. (17.)]

1642. A Short History of the Anabaptists of High and Low Germany, etc. 4°, pp. iv, 56.   12
B. M. [E. 148. (5.)]

1642. [R. B.] — An Answer to the Treatise of P. B. [no. 6] on Baptisme, etc. 4°.   13

1642. A Warning for England, especially for London, in the famous history of the frantic Anabaptists,   14
etc. 4°.
Bodleian, [Wood. 647. 2.]

1642. Reasons humbly offered in justification of the action of letting a Room in London-house unto certain   15
peaceable Christians called Anabaptists. 4°.
Bodleian, [4°, P. 1. Art. BS.]

1642. J. TAYLOR. — A Cluster of Coxcombes: or a Cinquepace of five sorts of Knaves and Fooles: 16
namely, the Donatists, Publicans, Disciplinarians, Anabaptists, and Brownists, etc. [n. pl.] 4°,
pp. 8.
B. M. [E. 154. (49.)]

1643. The Roundheads Catechisme: or, the Newter catechizing the Anabaptists, Puritans, Separatists,   17
[9 Apr.] and well-affected under the name of Roundheads, with their joynt Answer to the same. 32°,
pp. 32.
B. M. [E. 1205. (1.)]

1643. [P. B.][ARBON] — A Reply to the Frivolous and impertinent Answer of R. B. [no. 13] to the   18
[14 Apr.] Discourse of P. B. [no. 6] in which Discourse is shewed, that the Baptisme in the Defection of
Antichrist, is the ordinance of God, notwithstanding the corruptions that attend the same, and that
the Baptisme of Infants is lawful; both of which are vindicated from the exceptions of R. B. and
further cleared by the same author [i. e. P. B.]. There is also a reply in way of Answer to some
exceptions of E. B. [no. 8] against the same. 4°, pp. vi, 64.
B. M. [E. 96. (20.)]

1643. An Anabaptists Sermon. Preached at the Rebaptizing of a Brother, at the new or holy Jordan, as   19
[19 Apr.] they call it, neare Bow or Hackney River, etc. 4°, pp. 4.
B. M. [E. 97. (13.)]

1643. [S. C.] — A Christian Plea for Christians Baptisme: Raised from the grave of *Apostasie*: or, A   20
[25 May] Short Treatise, being a reproof of some things written by A. R. in his Treatise entituled *The Van-
itie* [no. 9], etc. 4°, pp. viii, 30.
B. M. [E. 104. (2.)]

1643. The Clergyes Bill of Complaint; or submissive suit of one in the behalf of all the Orthodox and   21
great sorrow-suffering Church-men throughout England; exhibited to the Houses of Parliament
against Brownists, Anabaptists, and other Schismaticks. Oxford, 4°.
Bodleian, [Pamph. 58.]

1643. [S. C.] — A Christian Plea for Infants Baptisme, or a Confutation of some things written by A. R.   22
[8 Feb.] in his Treatise entituled *The Second Part* [no. 10] etc. 4°, pp. ii, 166.
B. M. [E. 32. (2.)]

1643. T. BLAKE. — The Birth-Priviledge or Covenant-Holinesse of Beleevers and their Issue in the time   23
[18 Mar.] of the Gospel: With the right of Infants to Baptism. 4°, pp. vi, 34.
B. M. [E. 37 (29.)]

1644. The Anabaptists Groundwork for Reformation: or, New Planting of Churches, that no man,   24
[31 May] woman nor child, may be baptized, but such as have justifying Faith, and doe make profession
thereof, before, to the Baptizer, Found false, with all things depending thereon, as being contrary
to the Scriptures, and to the Examples of Christ and his Apostles, etc. 4°, pp. iv, 34.
B. M. [E. 50. (2.)]

1644. H. AINSWORTH. — A Seasonable Discourse, or, a Censure upon a Dialogue of the Anabaptists, etc.   25
[4 June] 4°, pp. iv, 74. [first printed (probably) in 1623.]
B. M. [E. 50. (8.)]

1644. T. BAKEWELL. — A Confutation of the Anabaptists, and all others who affect not civill government;   26
[21 June] proving the Lawfulnesse of it . . . Also Arguments against the Anabaptists, proving that Infants
borne of Christian Parents ought to be baptized, etc. 4°, [n. p.] pp. 102.
B. M. [E. 51. (20.)]

1644. T. NUTT. — The Nut-Cracker crackt by the Nutt . . . being the vindication of honest men from   27
[3 Aug.] the scandalous aspersions of T. B. as you may see in his learned book called the *Confutation* [no.
26], etc. large 4°, [n. p.] pp. 8.
B. M. [E. 254. (11.)]

1644. S. MARSHALL. — A Sermon of the Baptizing of Infants; preached in the Abbey-Church at West-   28
[27 Aug.] minster. 4°, pp. iv, 62.
B. M. [K. P. gold no. 171. (21.)]

1644. Infants Baptizing Proved Lawfull by the Scriptures: Objections against it resolved and removed, etc. 4°, pp. 16. 29
[13 Sept.] B. M. [E. 8. (31.)]

1644. W. COOKE. — A learned and Full Answer to a Treatise intituled *The Vanity* [nos. 9 & 10], etc. Also the question concerning the necessitie of Dipping in Baptisme is fully discussed, etc. 4°, pp. viii, 112. 30
[16 Sept.] B. M. [E. 9. (2.)]

1644. John the Baptist, Forerunner of Christ Iesvs; or A necessity for Liberty of Conscience, as the only meanes under heaven to strengthen Children weake in faith, to convince Hereticks misled in faith, etc. 4°, pp. viii, 108. 31
[23 Sept.] B. M. [E. 9. (13.)]

1644. F. CORNWELL. — The Vindication of the Royall Commission of King Jesus, Matt. xxviii: 18-20, compared with Mark, xvi: 15, 16, against the Antichristian Faction of Pope Innocensius the third, that enacted by a decree that the Baptisme of the Infants of Beleivers should succeed Circumcision. 4°, pp. vi, 18. 32
[27 Sept.] B. M. [E. 10. (15.)]

1644. The Summe of a Conference at Terling in Essex, Jan. 11, 1643 . . . on Infants Baptisme, etc. 4°, pp. viii, 36. 33
[7 Oct.] B. M. [E. 12. (2.)]

1644. A Declaration against Anabaptists: to stop the Persecution fō their errours, falsely pretended to be a *Vindication* [no. 32], etc. 4°, pp. ii, 6. 34
[9 Oct.] B. M. [E. 12. (9.)]

1644. The Confession of Faith of those Churches which are commonly (though falsely) called Anabaptists, etc. 4°, pp. 24. 35
[16 Oct.] B. M. [E. 12. (24.)]

1644. To Sions Virgins: Or, A Short Forme of Catechisme of the Doctrine of *Baptisme*, in use in these Times that are so full of Questions. By an Ancient Member, of that long agoe gathered Congregation, whereof Mr. *Henry Jacob* was an Instrument of gathering it, and the Pastour worthy of double honour, Mr. *John Lathroppe* succeeding him, now pastor in *New-England:* and the beloved Congregation, through Gods mercies sees her Teachers, waiting when God shall give more Liberty and Pastours according to his own heart, praying the Lord of the harvest to thrust forth Labourers into his harvest. 4°, pp. iv, 8. 36
[4 Nov.] B. M. [E. 17. (19.)]

1644. T. BAKEWELL. — The Antinomians Christ Confounded, and the Lords Christ exalted, [pp. 56-68. "The grounds of true Religion laid open and applied"] etc. 4°, pp. iv, 68. 37
[19 Nov.] B. M. [E. 17. (16.)]

1644. The New Distemper, written by the Author of the *Loyall Convert*, etc. Oxford, 4°, pp. ii, 26. 38
[30 Nov.] B. M. [E. 17. (20.)]

1644. [T. B., B. D.] — A Moderate answer to these two Questions: (1) whether ther be sufficient ground in Scripture to warrant . . . a Christian to present his infant to the Sacrament of Baptism; (2) whether it be not sinfull . . . to receiv the Sacrament in a mixt assembly. 4°, pp. ii, 32. 39
[28 Nov.] B. M. [E. 19. (6.)]

1644. C. BLACKWOOD. — The Storming of Antichrist in his strongest Garrisons, of compulsion of Conscience, and Infants Baptisme, etc. 4°, pp. iv, 62, 68. 40
[28 Dec.] B. M. [E. 22. (15.)]

[1644.] J. SPILSBURY. — A Treatise concerning the lawful subjects of Baptism, etc. 4°. [probably 1st ed. of no. 149.] 41

1644. T. LAMB. — The Un-Lawfulnesse of Infants Baptisme, etc. 4°. 42

1644. The Compassionate Samaritane. Vnbinding the Conscience, and powring oyle into the wounds which have beene made upon the Separation, etc. [pp. 60-71 the Anabaptists in particular.] 24°, pp. 84. 43
B. M. [E. 1202. (1.)]

1644. The Fountaine of Free Grace opened . . . wherein they [*i. e.* the Congregation of Christ in London falsly called Anabaptists] vindicate themselves from the scandalous aspersions of holding *Free-Will*, and denying a free *Election* by grace. 12°, pp. iv, 24. 44
[21 Jan.] B. M. [E. 1181. (3.)]

1644. I. KNUTTON. — Seven Qvestions abovt the Controversie betweene the Chvrch of England, and the Separatists and Anabaptists, breifely discussed, etc. 4°, pp. iv, 36. 45
[31 Jan.] B. M. [E. 25. (20.)]

1644. D. FEATLEY. — The Dippers Dipt, or the Anabaptists dvck'd and plvng'd over Head and Eares at a Disputation in Southwark, etc. 4°, pp. xviii, 228. 46
[7 Feb.] B. M. [E. 268. (11.)]

1644. [P. B.] — A Defence of the Lavvfulnesse of Baptizing Infants ... in way of answer to something written by J. Spilsberie [no. 41], etc. 4°, pp. vi, 64.
[22 Feb.]
B. M. [E. 270. (12.)] 47

1644. S. Richardson. — Some brief Considerations on Dr. Featley, his book intituled *The Dipper Dipt,* [no. 46], wherein in some measure is discovered his many great and false accusations of divers persons commonly called *Anabaptists,* etc. 4°, pp. ii, 18.
[25 Feb.]
B. M. [E. 270. (22.)] 48

1645. H. Denne. — Antichrist Vnmasked in two Treatises. The first, An Answer unto two Pædobaptists ... the Arguments for Childrens Baptisme opened, and answered. The Second, the Man of Sinne discovered in Doctrine, etc. 4°, pp. iv, 52.
[1 Apr.]
Bodleian, [G. Pamph. 1042. (4.)] 49

1645. R. Ram. — Pædobaptisme: or, the Baptizing of Infants Justified, by the judgment and practice of ancient and modern Divines, etc. 4°, pp. iv, 28.
[3 Apr.]
B. M. [E. 276. (12.)] 50

1645. [J. G.] (Raunt.) — Truth's Victorie against Heresie; all sorts comprehended under those ten mentioned, viz.: (1) Papists; (2) Familists; (3) Arrians; (4) Arminians; (5) Anabaptists; (6) Separatists; (7) Antinomists; (8) Monarchists; (9) Millenarists; (10) Independents, etc. 4°, pp. iv, 74.
[9 Apr.]
B. M. [E. 277. (7.)] 51

1645. [R. Byfield.] — Temple-defilers defiled, wherein a true visible Church of Christ is described, the evils and pernicious errours, especially appertaining to Schisme, Anabaptisme and Libertinisme that infest our Church are discovered, etc. 4°, pp. viii, 40.
[22 Apr.]
B. M. [E. 278. (20.)] 52

1645. T. Blake. — Infants baptisme freed from Anti-christianisme. A full repulse to Mr. C. B. in his assault. *The Storming* [no. 40], etc. 4°, pp. viii, 130.
[29 Apr.]
B. M. [E. 279. (10.)] 53

1645. E. Pagitt. — Heresiography: or, a description of the Hereticks and Sectaries of these latter times, etc. 4°, pp. xxiv, 132.
[8 May]
B. M. [E. 282. (5.)] 54

1645. G. Phillips. — A Reply to a Confutation of some Grounds for Infant Baptism; as also concerning the form of a Church, put forth against me by one T. Lamb [no. 42?], etc. 4°, pp. xvi, 154.
[10 June]
B. M. [E. 287. (4.)] 55

1645. W. Kiffin. — A Briefe Remonstrance of the Reasons and Grounds of Anabaptists for their Separation, etc. 4°, pp. iv, 16.
[26 July]
B. M. [E. 293. (16.)] 56

1645. J. Ricraft. — A Looking Glasse for the Anabaptists and the rest of the Separatists: Wherein they may clearly behold a brief Confutation of a certain un-licensed Scandalous Pamphlet Intituled the *Remonstrance* [no. 56], etc. 4°, pp. iv, 26.
[4 Sept.]
B. M [E. 299. (9.)] 57

1645. J. Brinsley. — The Doctrine and Practice of Pædo-baptisme asserted and vindicated. 4°, pp. vi, 100, 86.
[10 Sept.]
B. M. [E. 300. (14.)] 58

1645. The Anabaptists Catechisme: with all their Practises, Meetings and Exercises, etc. 16°, pp. ii, 14.
[11 Sept.]
B. M. [E. 1185. (8.)] 59

1645. [Capt. Hobson.] — The Fallacy of Infants Baptisme Discovered, or Five Arguments, to prove that Infants ought not to be baptized, etc. 4°, pp. vi, 16.
[10 Dec.]
B. M. [E. 311. (18.)] 60

1645. J. Tombes. — Two Treatises and an Appendix to them concerning Infant-Baptisme: (1) an Exercitation presented to the Chairman of a Committee of the Assembly; (2) an Examen of Mr. Marshalls Sermon [no. 28], etc. 4°, pp. x, 34, 176, x.
[16 Dec.]
B. M. [E. 312. (1.)] 61

1645. R. Fage, Jr. — The Lawfulnesse of Infants-Baptisme, or, An Answer to Thomas Lamb his eight arguments entituled *The Un-lawfulnesse* [no. 42], etc. 16°, pp. ii, 16.
[16 Dec.]
B. M. [E. 1189. (10.)] 62

1645. A Declaration concerning the Publike Dispute which should have been in the Publike meeting-house of Alderman-bury, the 3d of this inst. moneth of December, concerning Infants-Baptisme, etc. by H. Cox, H. Knollys, W. Kiffin, etc. 4°, pp. ii, 20.
[20 Dec.]
B. M. [E. 313. (22.)] 63

1645. J. Mabbatt. — A Briefe or Generall Reply unto Mr. Knuttons Answers unto the VII. Questions [no. 45] and the Controversie between the Church of England and the Separatist and Anabaptist, briefly discussed, etc. [n. pl.] 4°, pp. 40.
[I have it.] 64

1645. J. WAITE. — The Way to Heaven by Water, concomitated by the sweet-breathing gales of the Spirit. York, 4°. Bodleian, [Mason. AA. 473.]   65

1645. R. GARNER. — A Treatise of Baptisme; wherein is clearly proved the lawfulnesse of Beleevers Baptisme, etc 4°, pp. iv, 34. B. M. [E. 314. (16.)]   66
[3 Jan.]

1645. C. BLACKWOOD. — Apostolicall Baptisme: or a Sober Rejoinder to a Treatise written by Mr. T. Blake, intituled *Infants Baptisme freed* [no. 53], etc. 4°, pp. iv, 83, iii. B. M. [E. 315. (17.)]   67
[13 Jan.]

1645. [R. J.] — Nineteen Arguments, proving Circumcision no seal of the Covenant of Grace ... the unlawfullnesse of Infant Baptisme, etc. 4°, pp. iv, 20. B. M. [E. 315. (16.)]   68
[13 Jan.]

1645. J. SALTMARSH. — The Smoke in the Temple, etc. 4°, pp. xvi, 32, 70. B. M. [E. 316. (14.)]   69
[16 Jan.]

1645. [T. B.][AKEWELL.] — A Justification of two points now in controversie with the Anabaptistes, etc. 4°, pp. ii, 30. Bodleian, [C. 13. 16. Linc.]   70
[19 Jan.]

1645. R. BAYLIE. — A Dissvasive from the Errours of the Time, etc. 4°, pp. xxiv, 252. B. M. [E. 317. (15.)]   71
[22 Jan.]

1645. R. WILLIAMS. — Christenings make not Christians, or, a Briefe Discourse concerning that name *Heathen*, commonly given to the Indians. As also concerning that great point of their Conversion, etc. 16°, pp. ii, 22. B. M. [E. 1189. (8.)]   72
[25 Jan.]

1645. A Confession of Faith of Seven Congregations, or Churches of Christ in London, which are commonly (but uniustly) called Anabaptists, etc. Second Impression, corrected and enlarged [see no. 35]. 4°, [n. p.] pp. 24. B. M. [E. 319. (13.)]   73
[28 Jan.]

1645. H. KNOLLYS. — The Shining of a Flaming Fire in Zion. Or, a Clear Answer unto 13 Exceptions against the Grounds of New Baptism; (so called) in Mr. Saltmarsh his Book intituled *The Smoke* [no. 69], etc. 4°, pp. iv, 18. B. M. [E. 322. (16.)]   74
[11 Feb.]

1645. J. EACHARD. — The Axe against Sin and Error, and the Truth conquering, etc. 4°, pp. xii, 40. B. M. [E. 322. (26.)]   75
[14 Feb.]

1645 T. EDWARDS. — *Gangræna*: or a Catalogue and Discovery of many of the Errours, Heresies, Blasphemies and pernicious Practices of the Sectaries of this time, vented and acted in England in these four last yeares, etc. 4°, pp. xxiv, 184. [first part.] B. M. [E. 323. (2.)]   76
[16 Feb.]

1645. N. HOMES. — A Vindication of Baptizing Beeleevers Infants, in some Animadversions upon Mr. Tombes, His *Exercitations about Infant Baptism* [no. 61], etc. 4°, pp. vi, 227, v. B. M. [E. 324. (1.)]   77
[20 Feb.]

1645. J. GEREE. — *Vindiciæ Pædo-baptismi:* or a Vindication of Infant Baptism, in a full Answer to Mr. Tombs his twelve arguments alleged against it [no. 61?], etc. 4°, pp. viii, 72. B. M. [E. 325. (25.)]   78
[4 Mar.]

1646. S. MARSHALL. — A Defence of Infant-Baptism: in answer to two Treatises of Mr. J. Tombes [no. 61], etc. 4°, pp vi, 256, iv. B. M. [E. 332. (5.)]   79
[9 Apr.]

1646. J. LEY. — Light for Smoak, or a reply to *The Smoke in the Temple* [no. 69], etc. 4°, pp. xxx, 98, 22. B. M. [E. 333. (2.)]   80
[11 Apr.]

1646. J. SPILSBURY. — Gods Ordinance, the Saints Priviledge: discovered and proved in two Treatises ... the second wherein the Saints right to the use of Baptisme is proved, etc. 4°, pp. viii, 80. B. M. [E. 335. (17.)]   81
[4 May]

1646. T. BAKEWELL. — An Answer, or Confutation, of divers Errors Broached and Maintained by the seven Churches of Anabaptists, contained in their *Confession* [no. 73], and other grosse opinions held by them against the cleare Light of the Gospel, etc. 4°, pp. iv, 46. B. M. [E. 336. (10.)]   82
[7 May]

1646. T. EDWARDS. — The Second Part of *Gangræna* [see no. 76], or a fresh and further Discovery of the Errors, Heresies, Blasphemies, and dangerous Proceedings of the Sectaries of this time, etc. 4°, pp. xii, 212. B. M. [E. 338. (12.)]   83
[28 May]

1646. W. HUSSEY. — An Answer to Mr. Tombes his sceptical Examination [Exercitation] of Infant-Baptisme [no. 61], etc. 4°, pp. vi, 72. B. M. [E. 343. (3.)]   84
[6 July]

1646. H. LAVOR. — Predestination handled and maintained against Papists, Arminians, and Certaine 85
[10 July] Churches also of Anti-pædobaptists. 12°, pp. ii, 34.
B. M. [E. 1137. (2.)]

1646. Of Baptisme. The heads and order of such things as are especially insisted on, you will find in the 86
[10 Aug.] table of Chapters. Rotterdam, 16°, pp. viii, 410, vi.
B. M. [E. 1116.]

1646. J. TOMBES. — An Apology or Plea for the Two Treatises and Appendix concerning Infant Baptism 87
[28 Aug.] [no. 61], etc. 4°, pp. vi, 158.
B. M. [E. 352. (1.)]

1646. T. GATAKER. — Shadowes without Substance, or, pretended New Lights, etc. 4°, pp. ii, 116. 88
[11 Sept.] B. M. [E. 366. (2.)]

1646. J. COTTON. The Grovnds and Endes of the Baptisme of the Children of the Faithfvll, etc. 4°, 89
[10 Oct.] pp. viii, 196.
B. M. [E. 356. (16.)]

[1646.] [R. H.] — The True Guide, etc. [a discourse on Baptism.] [see no. 91.] 4°. 90

1646. [R. B.] — A Briefe Answer to R. H. his Booke, entitled *The True Guide* [no. 90], etc. 4°, pp. ii, 38. 91
[12 Oct.] B. M. [E. 357. (2.)]

[1646.] [MR.] HARRISON. — Pædobaptism Oppugned, etc. [in review of no. 78, as see no. 98], etc. 4°. 92

1646. [A. WYKE.] — The Innocent in Prison Complaining; or, a True Relation of the Proceedings of the 93
Committee of Ipswich, the Committee at Bury St. Edmonds, in the County of Suffolk, against one
Andrew Wyke, a witness of Jesus in the same County, who was committed to prison, June 3, 1646,
etc. [*Crosby*, i: 235.]

1646. W. HUSSEY. — A lvst Provocation of Master Tombes, to make good his generall charge [no. 87?] 94
[14 Oct.] against Mr. W. Hussey's Satisfaction to his Scepticall Exercitation [no. 84], etc. 4°, pp. iv, 8.
B. M. [E. 357. (6.)]

1646. [T. KILCOP.] — Seekers Supplyed, or Three-and-Forty Non-Church Queries by Scripture answered. 95
[2 Nov.] Penned and Publish't for the vindication of Christs commands, and edification and confirmation of
his people, by T. K. Servant to Christ Jesus, the King of Kings. 4°, pp. iv, 12.
B. M. [E. 359. (4.)]

[1646.] [J. WILKINSON.] — The Sealed Fountaine opened to the faithfull, and their Seed. Or, a short 96
[17 Nov.] Treatise, shewing that some Infants are in the state of Grace, and capable of the *Seales*, and
others not. Being the chief point wherein the *Separatists* doe blame the *Anabaptists*. By J. W.
Prisoner at Colchester against John Morton, Prisoner at London. 32°, pp. xii, 16.
B. M. [E. 1205. (2.)]

1646. F. SPANHEMIUS. — Englands VVarning by Germanies Woe: or, An Historicall Narration of the 97
[28 Nov.] Originall, Progresse, Tenets, Names, and Severall Sects of the Anabaptists, in Germany and the
Low Countries, etc. 4°, pp. ii, 50.
B. M. [E. 362. (28.)]

1646. J. GEREE. — *Vindicia Vindiciarum*; or, a Vindication of his *Vindication of Infant Baptism* 98
[27 Nov.] [no. 78] from the exceptions of Mr. Harrison in his *Pædobaptism Oppugned* [no. 92], etc. and
from the exceptions of Mr. Tombes [no. 87], etc. 4°, pp. vi, 42.
B. M. [E. 363. (13.)]

1646. T. EDWARDS. — The Third Part of *Gangræna*, etc. [see nos. 76 & 83.] 4°, pp. xlii, 318. 99
[28 Nov.] B. M. [E. 368. (5.)]

1646. B. COXE. — An Appendix to a Confession of Faith, or a more full Declaration of the Faith and Judg- 100
[30 Nov.] ment of Baptized Beleevers. Occasioned by the inquiry of some wel-affected and godly persons
in the Country. Published for the cleering of truth and discovery of their mistake who have
imagined a dissent in fundamentals where there is none. 4°, pp. 12.
B. M. [E. 364. (1.)]

1646. An Order of the Lords assembled in Parliament, for the punishing of Anabaptists and Sectaries that 101
[22 Dec.] shall disturbe the ministers in their publike exercises, etc. 4°, pp. ii, 4.
B. M. [E. 367. (2.)]

1646. R. BAYLIE. — Anabaptism the True Fovntaine of Independency, Brownisme, Antinomy, Familisme, 102
[4 Jan.] and most of the other Errours, which for the Time doe trouble the Church of England . . . Also
the Questions of Pædobaptisme and Dipping handled from Scripture. In a second Part of the
Disswasive [no. 71], etc. 4°, pp. xxxii, 179, xiii.
B. M. [E. 369. (9.)]

1646. A Catalogue of the severall sects and opinions in England, and other nations, with a brefe Rehersall 103
[19 Jan.] of their false and dangerous tenets. single sheet fol. [refers to "Anabaptists."]
B. M. [669. f. 10. (111.)]

1646. O. SEDGWICK. — The Natvre and Danger of heresies; opened in a sermon before the House of 104
[27 Jan.] Commons [on Rev. xii: 15, 16], etc. 4°, pp. iv, 44.
B. M. [E. 372. (13.)]

1646. The New Letanie, etc. Broad sheet, folio. [refers to "Anabaptists," etc.] 105
[15 Mar.] B. M. (669. f. 10. (120.))

1646. R. Whittle. — An Answer to Mr. F. Cornwells Positions and Inferences, concerning Dipping, 106
[24 Mar.] Anabaptisme, Antipædobaptisme, Tythes and Consecrated Churches, etc. 4°, pp. ii, 22.
B. M. [E. 516. (1.)]

1647. The Anabaptists late Protestation; or, their Resolvtion to depart the City of London. Wherein is 107
[2 Apr.] set forth the full proceedings of a great number of Anabaptists, at a late Conventicle neere Old-Street, etc. 4°, [n. p.] pp. 8.
B. M. [E. 383. (11.)]

1647. J. Bastwick. — The Storming of the Anabaptists garrisons, with a brief Discovery of the weak- 108
[8 June] nesse of the same, etc. 4°, pp. ii, 50.
B. M. [E. 390. (23.)]

1647. G. Palmer. — Sectaries vnmasked and confuted, by the treating upon divers Points of doctrine in 109
[6 July] debate betwixt the Presbyterians and Sectarists, Anabaptists, Independents and Papists, etc. 4°,
pp. viii, 56.
B. M. [E. 396. (27.)]

1647. G. Palmer. — The Voice of Infants by Infants Defender, etc. 4°, pp. 12. 110
[6 July] B. M. [E. 396. (28.)]

1647. A Declaration by Congregationall Societies in and about London; as well of those commonly called 111
[22 Nov.] Anabaptists, as others, in way of vindication of themselves touching: (1) Liberty; (2) Magistracy; (3) Propriety; (4) Polygamie, etc. 4°, pp. 14.
B. M. [E. 416. (20.)]

[1647.] A Looking-Glass for Sectaryes; or, True Newes from Newbery, being the relation of the Newbery 112
Anabaptistes, whereof three were to be carried into Heaven, but failed in their Iourney, etc.
4°, pp. 8.
B. M. [E. 419. (20.)]

1647. H. Grotius. — Baptizatorum Puerorum Institutio, etc. Londini, 12°. [Watt, s. n.] 113

1647. J. Hoornbeek. — Disputationes de Baptismo Veterum, etc. Ultraject. 4°. [Watt, s. n.] 114

1647. A Testimony to the Truth of Jesus Christ, and to our Solemn League and Covenant; as also against 115
[18 Jan.] the Errours, Heresies and Blasphemies of these times, etc. [p. 18 discusses " Errours against the Sacrament of Baptisme."] 4°, pp. ii, 38.
B. M. [E. 423. (3.)]

1647. [W. Dell.] — Baptismōn Didachē: or, The Doctrine of Baptismes, Reduced from its Ancient and 116
[19 Feb.] Moderne Corruptions: and restored to its Primitive Soundnesse and Integrity, etc. 4°, pp. iv, 26.
B. M. [E. 427. (25.)]

1648. T. Cobbet. — A Jvst Vindication of the Covenant and Church-estate of Children of Church-mem- 117
bers: as also of their right unto Baptisme . . . Hereunto is annexed a Refutation of a certain
Pamphlet, styled the Plain and wel-grounded Treatise [no. 1], etc. 4°, pp. xii, 296.
Bodleian, [4°, B. 9. Th. BS.]

1648. J. Church. — The Divine Warrant for Infant Baptism; or, Six Arguments for the Baptism of the 118
Infants of Christians, etc.
Bodleian, [Pamph. 87.]

1648. A. Mingzeis. — A Confutation of the Nevv Presbyterian Error, shewing not onely how neere our 119
late Presbyterians came to the Anabaptists in restrayning the Supper of the Lord from the people
by way of Examination, as they doe children from the Sacrament of Baptisme, etc. 16°, pp. 24.
B. M. [E. 1181. (10.)]

[1648.] [W. Cooke.] — The Font uncovered, for Infant-Baptisme, etc. 4°. 120

1648. R. Allen. — An Antidote against Heresy; or a Preservative for Protestants against the poyson of 121
Papists, Anabaptists, Arrians, Arminians, etc. and their pestilent errours, etc. 16°, pp. xviii, 144.
B. M. [E. 1168. (2.)]

[1648.] S. Oates. — A New Baptisme and Ministery, etc. 4°. 122

1649. The Humble Petition and Representation of several Churches of God in London, commonly (though 123
[3 Apr.] falsly) called Anabaptists. [presented to Parliament 2 Apr.] with the Answer thereto. 4°, pp. 8.
B. M. [E. 549. (14.)]

1649. J. Drew. — A Serious Addresse to Samuel Oates for a Resolve in some few Quæries touching his 124
[6 Apr.] New Baptisme and Ministery [no. 122], etc. 4°, pp. 38.
B. M. [E. 549. (16.)]

1649. Eight Reasons for Baptizing Infants born of Believing Parents, etc. 4°, p. ii, 8. 125
[13 June] B. M. [E. 559. (18.)]

1649. T. HOOKER.—The Covenant of Grace Opened: Wherein these particulars are handled; viz.: 126
[2 July] (1) What the Covenant of Grace is; (2) What the Seales of the Covenant are; (3) Who are the Parties and Subjects fit to receive these Seales. From all which Particulars Infants Baptisme is proved and vindicated, etc. 4°, pp. ii, 86.
[Hon. J. Hammond Trumbull.]

1649. *Ecclesiæ Gemitus sub Anabaptistica Tyrannide.* [n. pl.] 8°, pp. viii, 56. 127
B. M. [E. 1214. (2.)]

1649. Infants Baptism Maintained; or, a True Account of the Disputation at Ashford in Kent, Julie 27, 128
[3 Jan.] 1649 4°, pp. iv, 28.
B. M. [E. 587. (12)]

1649. P. CHAMBERLEN.—To my beloved Friends and Neighbours of the Blackfryers, etc. [single 129
[21 Feb.] sheet.] fol.
B. M. [fol. 9. (16.)]

[1649.] P. CHAMBERLEN.—A Question to Dr. Gouge whether that Sprinkling of Infants in Baptism is of 130
God or Man? 4°.

[1649.] W. HARTLY.—Infant Baptism none of Christs, etc. [cited and criticised by R. Carpenter, no. 191.] 131

1650. T. BAKEWELL.—The Dippers Plunged in a Sea of Absurdities. Or, An Answer to Dr. Chamberlen 132
concerning Sprinkling the Baptized [no. 130], etc. 4°, pp. 8.
B. M. [E. 605. (4.)]

1650. P. CHAMBERLEN.—Master Bakewells Sea of Absurdities concerning Sprinkling [no. 132] calmly 133
[12 Apr.] driven back, etc. 4°, pp. ii, 14.
B. M. [702. d. 12. (10.)]

1650. T. BAKEWELL.—Doctor Chamberlen visited with a Bunch of his own Grapes, gathered out of his 134
[13 May] Packet of Letters, etc. . . . Also, an Answer to Dr. Chamberlens Reply concerning Sprinkling the Baptized [no. 133], etc. 4°, pp. 28.
B. M. [E. 601. (4.)]

1650. R. BAXTER.—Plain Scripture Proof of Infants Church-Membership and Baptism, being the Argu- 135
ments prepared for (and partly managed in) the publick dispute with Mr. Tombes at Bewdley, on the 1st day of Jan. 1649, etc. 4°, pp. liv, 346.
B. M. [K. P. gold no. 685. (3.)]

1650. J. COUCH.—*Anabaptistorum Scrupuli:* or, Answer of a Kentish Anabaptist, made in the year 136
[4 Feb.] 1649. 4°, pp. viii, 30.
B. M. [E. 623. (2.)]

1650. N. STEPHENS.—A Precept for the Baptisme of Infants out of the New Testament, etc. 4°, pp. x, 62. 137
[10 Feb.] B. M. [E. 623. (9.)]

1650. R. EVERARD.—Baby-Baptisme Routed, etc. 4°. 138

1650. H. JESSEY.—A Store-house of provision to further resolution in several cases of conscience, and 139
questions now in dispute, etc. 8°. [*Crosby*, i: 322.]

1650. D. KING.—A Way in Sion, sought out, and found, for Believers to walk in, etc. . . . Wherein is 140
cleared up by Scripture and Arguments founded upon Scripture, who of right may administer Ordinances, and amongst the rest the Ordinance of Baptism with Water, etc. 4°. [*Ivimey*, ii: 577.]

1650. D. KING.—Some Beams of Light for the further clearing up of the Way; wherein crooked things 141
are made straight, and rough places made plain by direct Scriptures, etc. 4°. [*Ivimey*, ii: 578.]

1651. T. HALL.—The Font Guarded with XX Arguments, containing a Compendium of that Great 142
[20 Mar.] Controversie of Infant Baptism; Proving the lawfulness thereof, with a word to one Collier, and another to Mr. Tombes in the end of the Book. 4°, pp. xviii, 136.
B. M. [E. 658. (2.)]

1651. D. CAWDREY.—The Inconsistencie of the Independent way, with Scripture and It Self . . . with a 143
[16 May] Diatribe . . . concerning Baptism of Infants of Non-Confederate Parents, etc. 4°, pp. xxvi, 220.
B. M. [E. 629. (1.)]

1651. S. CHIDLEY.—The Separatists Answer to the Anabaptists Arguments concerning Baptism, or the 144
[22 Oct.] answer of S. C. to J. S.[pilsbury] concerning the point in difference, etc. 4°, [n. p.] pp. 16.
B. M. [E. 643. (22.)]

1651. G. FIRMIN —A Serious Question stated: viz. Whether the Ministers of England are bound by the 145
Word of God to Baptize the Children of all such Parents which say they believe in Jesus Christ, but refuse to submit to Church Discipline . . . The negative is defended, etc. 4°, pp. xxiv, 40.
B. M. [115. e. 5.]

1651. H. AINSWORTH.—A Seasonable Discourse. Or, a Censure upon a Dialogue of the Anabaptists, 146
etc. [first issued (probably) in 1623, and again in 1644 (no. 25).] 4°, pp. iv, 74.
Bodleian, [Pamph. 94.]

1652. Of Christs Testaments, viz : Baptisme and the Supper, etc. written in A. D. 1624 by Jacob Behm, 147
[22 May] and Englished by John Sparrow, etc. 4°, pp. xxvi, 98, x.
B. M. [E. 665. (4.)]

1652. The Disputes between Mr. Cranford and Dr. Chamberlen, at the house of Mr William Webb at the 148
[8 June] end of Bartholomew Lane by the Old Exchange 1 Mar. and 1, 6, 13 Apr. 1652. Published for the
satisfaction of all that love the truth. 4°, pp. vi, 28, iv.
B. M. [E. 666. (6.)]

1652. J. SPILSBURY. — A Treatise concerning the Lawful Subjects of Baptism, wherein are handled these 149
particulars: (1) Baptizing of Infants confuted; (2) the Covenant of Abraham hand'ed; (3) the
Baptism administered by an Antichristian power confuted: (4) how wanting church or ordinance
are to be recovered; (5) the Covenant, not Baptism, forms the Church: and how (6) there is no
succession under the New Testament, but such as is spiritually by faith in the Word of God.
[probably 2d ed. of no. 41.] 4°, pp. vi, 74.
B. M. [4323. b.]

1652. J. TOMBES. — *Præcursor;* or, a Forerunner to a large Review of the Dispute concerning Infant- 150
baptism 4°. [*Crosby,* i : 295.]

1652. C. BLACKWOOD. — A Brief Catechism concerning Baptism, first published at the end of his *Storm-* 151
ing [no. 40], etc. afterwards reprinted for the satisfaction and information of the people of God in
Lancashire, etc. 4°. [*Ivimey,* ii : 233.]

1652. J. TOMBES. — An Addition to the Apology for the two Treatises concerning Infant Baptisme [no. 152
87], etc. 4°.

1652. J. TOMBES. — Letters that passed between Mr. Baxter and Mr. Tombes concerning the Dispute [on 153
Infant Church Membership and Baptism]. 4°, pp. 14.
B. M. [K. P. gold no. 685. (3.)]

1652. H. LAWRENCE. — A Plea for the Vse of Gospell Ordinances, etc. against Mr. Dels Booke entituled 154
The Doctrine of Baptismes [no. 116], etc. 4°, pp. viii, 84.
B. M. [E. 654. (2.)]

1652. J. TAYLOR. — A Discourse on Baptism, its Institutions, and Efficacy upon all believers. 4°, pp. 155
[27 Nov.] iv, 60.
B. M. [E. 682. (2.)]

1652-4. J. TOMBES. — Anti-pædobaptism, or no plain . . . Scripture . . . Proof of Infants Baptism, etc. 156
[28 Nov.] 4°, pp. viii, 260. [Two parts.]
B. M. [E. 682. (3.)]

1652. D. CAWDREY. — A Sober Answer to a Serious Question propounded by Mr. G. Firmin, etc. whether 157
[10 Dec.] the Ministers of England are bound . . . to baptize [no. 145], etc. 4°, pp. viii, 32.
B. M. [E. 683. (23.)]

1652. T. GATAKER & S. WARD. — De Baptismatis Infantilis Vi & Efficacia Disceptatio. Privatim habita, 158
[25 Jan.] inter Virum celeberrimum D'num S. Wardum . . . et T. Gatakerum. 8°, pp. viii, 272.
B. M. [E. 1436. (1.)]

1652. W. ERBURY. — A Call to the Churches; or a Packet of Letters to the Pastors of Wales, presented 159
[19 Feb.] to the Baptized Teachers there, etc. 4°, pp. ii, 52.
B. M. [E. 688. (1.)]

1653. T. FULLER. — The Infants Advocate of Circumcision in Jewish and Baptism in Christian Children, 160
[2 May] etc. 8°, pp. xxii, 176, 40.
B. M. [E. 1431. (1.)]

1653. W. LYFORD. — An Apologie for our Publick Ministerie and Infant Baptism. Written som years ago 161
[10 May] for Private satisfaction of som Dissenting Brethren, etc. 4°, pp. vi, 46.
B. M. [E. 697. (9.)]

1653. J. SPITTLEHOUSE. — A Confutation of the Assertions of Mr. Samuel Oates (in relation to his not 162
[11 June] practising the laying on of hands on all baptized Believers) . . . who doth contrarywise affirm, etc.
4°, [no title p.] pp. 8.
B. M. [E. 699. (12.)]

1653. J. KELLETT, J. POMROY, P. GLISSON. — A Faithfvl Discovery of a treacherous Design of Mys- 163
[12 June] tical Antichrist displaying Christs Banners, etc. 4°, pp. viii, 60.
B. M. [E. 699. (13.)]

1653. H. HAGGAR. — The Foundation of the Font discovered to the view of all that desire to behold it, 164
[17 Aug.] and the baptizing of Men and Women when they believe (in rivers and fountains) proved to be a
standing Ordinance in the Church of Christ to the end of the world; by plain Scripture proof: in
answer to Mr. Cooke [no. 120], and Mr. Baxter [no. 135], etc. 4°, pp. viii, 132.
B. M. [E. 711. (1.)]

1653. G. BAITMAN. — The Arrow of the Almighty shot out of the creatures bowe against the uncalled 165
[9 Sept.] Ministers in England . . . likewise here is opened . . . the Mystery in Baptisme, etc. 4°,
pp. xii, 122.
B. M. [E. 712. (16.)]

1653. J. GOODWIN. — *Philadelphia;* or XL. Queries for the discovery of truth in this question; Whether 166
persons baptized after a profession of faith may hold communion with churches . . . baptized in
infancy? 4°, pp. 32.
B. M. [E. 702. (7.)]

1653. [W. A.] — An Answer to Mr. J. G.[oodwin] his XL. Queries, touching the Lawfulness or unlawful- 167
[21 Sept.] ness of holding church communion between such who have been baptized after their beleeving,
and others who have not otherwise been baptized then in their Infancie [no. 166], etc. 4°, pp. 96.
B. M. [E. 713. (17.)]

1653. W. KAYE. — Baptism without Bason: or, Plain Scripture-proof against Infant Baptism, etc. 4°, 168
[14 Nov.] pp. x, 42.
B. M. [E. 715. (13.)]

1653. J. GOODWIN — Water-dipping no Firm Footing for Church communion, etc. 4°, pp. 92. 169
[12 Dec.] B. M. [E. 723. (15.)]

1653. A False Jew; or, a wonderful Discovery of a Scot. Baptized at London for a Christian, circumcised 170
[15 Dec.] at Rome to act a Jew, re-baptized at Hexham for a Believer, but found out at Newcastle to be a
Cheat: Being a true Relation of the detecting of one Thomas Ramsey, born of Scotch parents at
London, etc. 4°, pp viii, 14, xiv.
B. M. [E. 724. (6.)]

1653. [T. TILLAM.] — Banners of Love displaied over the Church of Christ walking in the order of the 171
[16 Jan.] Gospel at Hexham . . . against the Jesuitical design lately attempted by the false Jew: or, an
Answer to a Narrative stuffed with untruths [no. 170], etc. 4°, pp. 48.
B. M. [E. 726. (8.)]

1653. C. SYDENHAM. — A Christian Sober and Plain Exercitation on the two grand practical Controver- 172
sies of these times; Infant Baptisme and Singing of Psalms. 8°, pp. vi, 210.
B. M. [E. 1443. (1.)]

1653. H. SAVAGE. — Tres Questiones Theologicæ in Comitiorum Vesperiis discussæ. An Pædobaptismus 173
sit licitus? Christus in quem baptizamur, sit Deus? Hæretici qua Hæretici, sint supplicio dam-
nandi? Oxon. 4°. [*Watt*, s. n.]

1653. J. TOMBES. — Refutatio Positionis, ejusque Confirmationis, Pædobaptismum esse licitum, affirman- 174
tis, ab Henrico Savage, S. T. D. [no. 173], etc. 4°. [*Crosby*, i: 295.]

1653. H. WHISTLER. — An Aim at an Upshot for Infant Baptism, etc. 4°. [*Watt*, s. n.] 175

1653. [H. D'ANVERS, E. CHILLENDEN, & *13 others*.] — Eight Questions in reference to that Principle of 176
the Foundation of the Doctrine of Christ, termed *Laying-on of Hands*, etc. 4°.

1653. J. MORE. — A Lost Ordinance Restored: or Eight Questions, etc. with a General Exhortation to 177
all Baptized Churches not yet under the Practice . . . of the laying on of hands, etc. 4°, pp. 8.
B. M. [E. 727. (1.)]

1653. J. HOORNBEEK. — Summa Controversiarum Religionis: cum Infidelibus, Hæreticis, Schismaticis: 178
Id est . . . Anabaptistis, etc. 8°, pp. xii, 1002, xiv.
B. M. [3559. a.]

1653. R. BYFIELD. — A Short Treatise describing the true Church of Christ, and the Evills of Schisme, 179
Anabaptism and Libertinism, etc. 4°, pp. ii, 40.
B. M. [T. 1562. (1.)]

1653. W. ALLEN. — Some Baptismal Abuses briefly discovered, etc. 4°, pp. xvi, 120. 180
B. M. [E. 702. (12.)]

1653. [W. E.][RBURY.] — The Madmans Plea; or, A Sober Defence of Capt. Chillingtons Church, etc. 181
4°, pp. ii, 10.
B. M. [E. 715. (17.)]

1653. E. PUNCLE. — A Cryer in the Wildernesse of England declaring the Baptisme of the Eternall Spirit 182
[21 Dec.] to be the onely Baptisme in Christs Kingdom, etc. 4°, pp. xii, 86.
B. M. [E. 725. (7.)]

1653. [J. H.][ORNE.] — *Diatribē Peri Paido-Baptismon:* or, a Consideration of Infant Baptism: Wherein 183
[13 Feb.] the Grounds of it are laid down, and the Validity of them discussed, and many things of Mr.
Tombes about it, etc. 4°, pp. viii, 160.
B. M. [E. 729. (3.)]

1654. J. TOMBES. — A public dispute betwixt J. Tombes respondent, J. Cragge and H. Vaughan, oppo- 184
nents, touching Infant Baptism . . . Also a sermon . . . by Mr. Cragge . . . wherein the necessity of dipping is refuted, and Infant Baptism asserted, etc. 8°.
B. M. [1355. a.]

1654. Anabaptists Anatomized and Silenced in a Public Dispute between J. Tombes, J. Cragge and H. 185
Vaughan Touching Infant Baptism, 5 Sept. 1653, etc. 8°, pp. xxii, 112.
B. M. [1355. a.]

1654. J. TOMBES. — A Plea for Anti-Pædobaptists against the Vanity and Falsehood of Scribled Papers 186
[20 May] entituled *The Anabaptists Anatomized* [no. 185], etc. 4°, pp. ii, 44.
B. M. [E. 738. (7.)]

1654. R. FARNWORTH. — To you that are called by the name of Baptists, or the Baptized people, etc. [no 187
[18 Aug.] title-page.] 4°, pp. 8.
B. M. [E. 809. (18.)]

1654. Conference Touchant Le Pedobaptesme, tenüe a Paris entre Le Sieur Jean Mestrezat, Pasteur de 188
[15 Sept.] l'Eglize Reformée de Charenton lés Paris & Theodore Naudin, docteur en medecine. Imprimé
a Londres, etc. 4°, pp. ii, 66.
B. M. [E. 812. (3.)]

1654. W. BRITTEN. — The Moderate Baptist; briefly shewing Scripture-way for that initiatory Sacrament 189
of Baptism, etc. Wherein may appear that the Baptists of our times hold not those strange opinions as many heretofore have done, etc. 4°. [*Crosby*, i: 254.]

1654. S. FORD. — Two Dialogues concerning the Practical Use of Infant Baptism, etc. 8°. [*Watt*, s. n.] 190

1654. R. CARPENTER. — The Anabaptist Washt and washt, and shrunk in the washing: Or, a Scholasticall Discussion of the much-agitated controversie concerning *Infant-Baptisme*; occasioned by a 191
Publike Disputation, Before a great assembly . . . in the Church of Newport-Pagnell: betwixt
Mr. *Gibs*, Minister there, and the author, etc. 16°, pp. xxvi, 470.
B. M. [E. 1484. (1.)]

1654. J. ROGERS. — Ohel, or Beth Shemesh: A Tabernacle for the Sun, or *Irenicum Evangelicum*, an 192
[7 Nov.] Idea of Church Discipline, etc. 4°, pp. xiv, 326, xlii.
B. M. [E. 717.]

1654. T. PATIENT. — The Doctrine of Baptisme, etc. 4°. 193
[Dr. Williams's Library.]

1654. R. BAYLIE. — The Disswasive [no. 71], etc. Vindicated from the Exceptions of . . . Mr. Tombes 194
[4 Jan.] [no. 152], etc. 4°, pp. iv, 88.
B. M. [E. 234. (7.)]

1655. J. READING. — Anabaptism Routed: or a Survey of the controverted points concerning: (1) Infant 195
[6 July] Baptisme; (2) Pretended Necessity of Dipping; (3) The dangerous Practice of Rebaptizing, etc.
4°, pp. xvi, 204.
B. M. [E. 845. (14.)]

1655. J. GOODWIN. — *Cata-Baptism;* or New Baptism waxing old, an answer to W. A. etc. 4°, pp. 196
[21 July] xcviii, 406, xviii.
B. M. [E. 849.]

1655. J. IVES. — Infant Baptism disproved, and Believers Baptism proved, being an answer to several 197
Arguments propounded by Mr. Alexander Kellie, and sent to him, etc. 4°. [*Crosby*, iv: 248.]

[1655.] S. FISHER. — Baby Baptism mere Babyism, etc. fol. [only *folio* in the controversy.] [*Crosby*, i: 198
363. *Ivimey*, ii: 248.]

1655. H. SAVAGE. — Thesis suæ Pædobaptismum esse licitum Defensio, contra J. Tombes [no. 174], etc. 199
Oxon. 4°. [*Watt*, s. n.]

1655. H. HAMMOND. — The Baptism of Infants defended, against the exceptions of Mr. Tombes, etc. 200
4°. [*Watt*, s. n.]

1655. W. ALLEN. — A Doubt resolved, or, Satisfaction for the Seekers [on Baptism, etc.] 4°, pp. ii, 38. 201
B. M. [4323. b.]

1655. J. PARNELL. — The Watcher: or the Stone cut out of the Mountain, etc. or a discovery of the 202
ground and end of all . . . seals, etc. 4°, pp. iv, 52.
B. M. [E. 845. (18.)]

1655. T. LAMB. — Truth Prevailing against the fiercest opposition; or, an Answer to Mr. I. Goodwins 203
Water Dipping [no. 169], etc. 4°, pp. xx, 128.
B. M. [4323. b.]

1655. S. FORD. — Dialogues on Infant Baptism, etc. 8°. 204
[21 Sept.] B. M. [K. P. gold no. 351. 18.]

1655. [H. WOODWARD.] — An Appeal to the Churches of Christ for their righteous judgment in the mat- 205
[13 Feb.] ters of Christ, etc. [as to Infant Baptism, etc.] [n. p.] 4°, pp. 44.
B. M. [E. 868. (6.)]

1656. M. MASON. — The Boasting Baptist dismounted, and the Beast disarmed and sorely wounded with- 206
[23 Apr.] out any carnal weapon, etc. 4°, pp. ii, 12. [the "Boasting Baptist" was Jonathan Johnson;
Mason, I judge, was a Quaker.]
B. M. [E. 877. (2.)]

1656. A Confession of the Faith of several [Baptist] Churches of Christ in the County of Somerset, and 207
[10 Aug.] of some Churches in the Counties neer adjacent, etc. 4°, pp. xviii, 40.
B. M. [E. 885. (6.)]

1656	[J. PENDARVIS] [et al.]—Sighs for Sion: or Faith and Love constraining some grievings in her Sorrow, and groanings for her Deliverance. By a few of her weak and unworthy children, etc. [*Ivimey*, ii: 64.]		208
1656.	J. CLOPPENBURGIUS.—*Gangræna Theologiæ Anabaptisticæ*, Disputationbus XLIIX. Et F. Spanhemii Diatriba historica de Origine, Progressu, & Sectis Anabaptistorum, etc. Franekeræ, 24°, pp. xvi, 436. B. M. [848. b. 11.]		209
1656.	Of Laying on of Hands, Heb. vi: 2, Or, a Discourse containing these 4 Chapters: (1) Ends of laying on of hands; (2) What it is not; (3) What it is; (4) That Christ never instituted it or commanded it as practised by some Baptized Believers, etc. 4°, pp. ii, 14. B. M. [700. g. 24. (2.)]		210
1656.	A True and Faithfull Narrative (for substance) of a Publique Dispute, between Mr. T. Porter and Mr. H. Haggar, concerning Infant Baptism, at Ellesmer, Salop, 30 Apr. 1656. 4°, pp. vi, 22. B. M. [E. 887. (1.)]		211
1656.	S. WINTER.—The Summe of diverse Sermons preached in Dublin ... wherein the Doctrine of Infant Baptism is asserted, and the main objections of Mr. Tombes [no. 156], etc. answered. Dublin, 8°, pp. xiv, 182. B. M. [4452. a.]		212
1656.	J. CRAGGE.— Arraignment and Conviction of Anabaptism against Mr. Tombes [no. 156], etc. 8°. Bodleian, [8°, N. 88. Th.]		213
1656. [8 Nov.]	*Eirēnikon*: a poeme, wherein is perswaded the composing of the differences of all the faithfull in Christ Jesus, under what form soever, whether Episcopall, Presbyterian, Congregationall, or Antipedobaptist. 4°, pp. 32. B. M. [E. 892. (6.)]		214
1657.	J. TOMBES.— Anti-Pædo-baptism; or The Third Part [see no. 156], etc. Being a full Review of the Dispute concerning Infant Baptism, etc. 4°, pp. xxviii, 932.		215
1657.	R. PURNELL.— A Little Cabinet richly stored, etc. ... Milk for Babes and Meat for strong Men, etc. 12°, pp. 468. [*Ivimey*, ii: 465.]		216
[1657.]	A Short Discovery of his Highness the Lord Protector's intentions touching the Anabaptists in the Army, and all such as are against his reforming things in the Church; which was first communicated to a Scotch Lord, who is called Twidle; but is now come to the ear of the Anabaptists: upon which there is propounded thirty-six queries for his Highness to answer to his own Conscience. By a well-wisher to the Anabaptists prosperity, etc. 4°. [*Crosby*, iii: 231.]		217
1657.	J. GOSNOLD.— *Baptismōn Didachē*: or, a discourse of the Baptism of Water and the Spirit, etc. 4°, ii, 43. B. M. [700. g. 21. (1.)]		218
1657.	J. WATTS.— A Scribe, Pharisee, Hypocrite and his Letter answered, Separates churched, Dippers sprinkled, or a Vindication of the Church and universities of England, etc. ... whereunto is added A narration of a publick dipping June 26, 1656, in a pond, etc. 4°, pp. lvi, 264, 212, viii, 120. B. M. [E. 921. (1.)]		219
1657.	S. FORD.— The Use of Infant Baptism, etc. 8°. Bodleian, [8°, G. 29. Th. BS.]		220
1658. [8 Nov.]	A. HOUGHTON.— An Antidote against H. Haggars poysonous pamphlet entituled *The Foundation* [no. 164], etc. 4°, pp. viii, 334. B. M. [E. 961. (1.)]		221
1658. [18 Dec.]	P. GUNNING & H DENNE.— A Contention for Truth. In two several publique Disputations ... concerning the Baptism of Infants, whether lawful or unlawful, etc. 4°, pp. vi, 46. B. M. [E. 963. (1.)]		222
1659.	J. TOMBES.— A Short Catechism about Baptism, etc. 8°, pp. 22. B. M. [E. 1854. (1.)]		223
1659.	J. TOMBES.— *Felo de se*; or, Mr. Baxters Self-Destroying, manifested in twenty arguments against Infant-baptism out of his own writings, etc. 4°. [*Crosby*, i: 296.]		224
1659.	S. PATRICK.— *Aqua Genitalis*: a Discourse concerning Baptism, etc. 12°. [on Acts xvi: 33.] [Dr. Williams's Library.]		225
1659.	A Disputation concerning Church-members and their Children in answer to xxi. Questions, by an Assembly of Divines at Boston in New England, etc wherein the state of such children when adult, together with their duty toward the Church, is discussed, etc. 4°. B. M. [K. P. gold no. 794 (3.)]		226
1659. [17 May]	Scripture Baptism and Church-Way with True Seekers. [n. pl. n. p.] 4°, pp. 24. B. M. [E. 954. (5.)]		227

1659.	Declaration of Several of the People called Anabaptists, in and about the City of London. [single sheet] fol. B. M. [816. m. 24. (9.)]	228
1659.	A Further Testimony to Truth; or, some Earnest Groans for a Righteous Settlement by some Baptized Congregations in Leicester, etc. [broadside.] [Mass. Histor. Society's Library.]	229
1659.	R. HUBBERTHORNE. — An Answer to a Declaration put forth by the general consent of the People called Anabaptists in . . . Loudon, etc. 4°, pp. 24. B. M. [4139. b.]	230
1659.	[J. FELL.] — The Interests of England stated; or, a Faithful and Just Account of the Aims of all Parties now prevailing; distinctly treating of the designments of the Roman Catholics, Royalists, Presbyterians, and Anabaptists, etc. 4°. [*Watt*, s. n.]	231
1659.	T. ASHTON. — Bloodthirsty Cyrus, unsatisfied with Blood; or, the boundless cruelty of an Anabaptist's Tyranny, manifested in a Letter of Col. J. Mason, Governor of Jersey, etc. 4°. [*Watt*, s. n.]	232
1659.	T. ASHTON. — Satan in Samuel's Mantle; or, the cruelty of Germany acted in Jersey; containing the arbitrary, bloody and tyrannical proceedings of John Mason, of a baptized Church, etc. 4°. [*Watt*, s. n.]	233
1659.	I. BOURNE. — Defence and Justification of Ministers maintenance by Tithes, Infant Baptism, Human Learning, etc. in reply to some Anabaptists, etc. 16°, pp. xvi, 98. B. M. [E. 1907. (1.)]	234
1659. [June]	J. ELLIS. — The Pastor and the Clerk: or a Debate (real) concerning Infant-Baptisme: wherein (1) the truth of that doctrine is (afresh) cleared; (2) The Scriptures alledged for it are vindicated; (3) The Objections usual are briefly answered; (4) and the Seeds-men of them truly Cyphered, etc. 16°, pp. xx, 208. B. M. [E. 1909. (2.)]	235
1659. [12 Sept.]	The Anabaptists Faith and Belief Opened, etc. [single sheet] fol. B. M. [669. f. 21. (72.)]	236
1659. [12 Jan.]	A Declaration of a small Society of Baptized Believers, undergoing the name of Free-Willers, about the city of London, etc. [s. sh.] fol. B. M. [669. f. 22. (67.)]	237
1659. [5 Jan.]	Anti-Quakerism; or a Character of the Quakers Spirit from its Original and First Cause. Written by a pious Gentleman that hath been thirteen years amongst the Separatists, etc. [s. sh.] fol. [B. M. [669. f. 22. (59.)]	238
1659. [12 Jan.]	H. ADIS. — A Fanaticks Mite cast into the Kings Treasury; being a Sermon Printed to the King, because not preached before the King. 4°, pp. xvi, 60. [contains appended the *Declaration* (no. 228), etc. of Adis's church.] B. M. [4473, aaa. 46. (1.)]	239
1659. [14 Jan.]	A Declaration of some of those People in or near London called Anabaptists who own and believe that Gods love in the death of his Son is extended to all men, and are in the practice of the Doctrines of Christ contained in Hebrews vi: 1, 2. folio, s. sh. B. M. [669. f. 22. (68.)]	240
1659. [28 Feb.]	A Serious Manifesto and Declaration of the Anabaptist, and other Congregational Churches, Touching the present Transactions of the Affairs of this Commonwealth, both in Church and State. [single sheet] fol. B. M. [669. f. 23. (65.)]	241
1659. [15 Mar.]	A Brief Confession or Declaration of Faith set forth by many of us, who are (falsely) called Anabaptists, to inform all men (in these days of scandal and reproach) of our innocent Belief and Practise, etc. 4°, pp. 12. B. M. [E. 1017. (14.)]	242
1659. [22 Mar.]	The Arraignment of the Anabaptists Good Old Cause, with the manner and proceedings of the Court of Justice against him, etc. 4°, pp. 16. B. M. [E. 1017. (32.)]	243
1659. [24 Mar.]	A Phanatique League and Covenant solemnly entered into by the Asserters of the Good Old Cause, etc. [single sheet] fol. B. M. [669. f. 24. (11.)]	244
1660. [26 Mar.]	The Character of a Phanatique, etc. [single sheet] fol. B. M. [669. f. 24. (34.)]	245
1660.	*Quesumus Te*, etc.: Or, the Supplement for the new Letany for these Times, etc. 4°, pp. 8. B. M. [E. 1017. (2.)]	246

1660. G. WHITEHEAD. — The Authority of the True Ministry, in Baptizing with the Spirit, etc. Being a short return to a Book entituled *A Reply to a Scandalous Paper*, subscribed by one Samuel Bradley, a Baptist Teacher, as concerning a dispute that was between some of the people called Quakers, and some Baptists in Southwarke, etc. 4°, pp. 16. [Smith's *Friends Books*, etc. ii : 887.]   247

1660. J. COLLENS. — A Message from the Spirit of the Lord to the Poeple called Anabaptists, etc. 4°. [*Watt*, s. n.]   248

1660. A Breife Description or Character of the Religion and Manners of the Phanatiques in Generall, etc. 16°, pp. ii, 52.
B. M. [E. 1765. (1.)]   249

1660. W. ALLEN. — A Retractation of Separation, wherein VI. Arguments formerly erected for the service of *Separation*, upon the account of *Infant Baptisme* are taken down; and VI. other arguments for saints generall communion . . . are erected in their room, etc. 4°, pp. vi, 72.
B. M. (4325. a.)   250

1660. R. BLOME. — The Fanatick History; or, an Exact relation and account of the old Anabaptists, and the New Quakers, etc. 8°, pp. x, 224.
B. M. [E. 1832. (2.)]   251

1660. A Brief Confession or Declaration of Faith (lately presented to King Charles the Second) set forth [26 July] by many of us who are (falsely) called Anabaptists, etc. [single sheet] fol.
B. M. [E. (fol.) 18. (63.)]   252

1660. G. PRESSICK. — A Briefe Relation of some of the most remarkable passages of the Anabaptists in [21 Nov.] High and Low Germany in the year 1521, etc. Dublin, 4°, pp. iv, 20.
B. M. [E. 1047. (5.)]   253

1660. The Humble Apology of some commonly called Anabaptists, in behalf of themselves and others of [28 Jan.] the same Judgment with them; With their *Protestation* against the late wicked and most horrid treasonable *Insurrection* and *Rebellion* acted in the City of London. Together with an *Apology* formerly presented to the Kings most Excellent Majesty, etc. 4°, pp. 18.
B. M. [E. 1057. (1.)]   254

1660. The Way to True Peace, or a Calm, Seasonable, and Modest Word in Love to the Independent Pha- [29 Jan.] naticks, Anabaptists, Presbyterians, Quakers, etc. 4°, pp. 8.
B. M. [E. 1057. (2.)]   255

1660. The Character of an Anabaptist. [single sheet] fol. [29 Jan.] B. M. [669. f. 26. (51.)]   256

1661. J. GOUGHE. — *Ecclesiæ Anglicanæ Threnodia*: in qua perturbatissimus Regni. et Ecclesiæ status sub Anabaptistica Tyrannide lugetur. 8°, pp. iv, 160.
B. M. [E. 1814. (2.)]   257

1661. H. ADIS. — A Fanaticks Alarm, given to the Mayor in his quarters by one of the Sons of Zion . . . H. A. a Baptized believer, undergoing the name of a Free-Willer, and also most ignominiously by the tongue of Infamy called a Fanatick, or a Mad Man. 4°, pp. 56.
B. M. [701. g. 45.]   258

1661. *Semper Iidem*: or, a Parallel betwixt the Ancient and Modern Fanaticks, etc. 4°, pp. 24.
Bodleian, [Pamph. 125.]   259

1661. J. GRIFFITH. — A Complaint of the Oppressed against the Oppressor. 4°. [*Taylor*, i: 244.]   260

1661. Thomas Venner, Orator Conventiculorum Regni Millenarii et Libertinorum, Seductor et Capitaneus Seditiosor, Anabaptistarum et Quackerorum in Civitat. Londinens. etc. 4°.
B. M. [K. 131. b. 23.]   261

1662. Behold a Cry; or, a True Relation of the inhuman and violent outrages of divers Soldiers, Consta- bles and others, practised upon many of the Lords people, commonly, tho' falsely called Anabap- tists, at their several meetings in and about London, etc. 8°. [*Crosby*, ii: 160.]   262

[1662.] [T. GRANTHAM.] — The Prisoner against the Prelate; or a Dialogue between the Common Gaol and Cathedral of Lincoln: wherein the true Faith and Church of Christ are briefly discovered and vindicated, by the authority of Scripture, Suffrages of Antiquity, Concessions and Confessions of the Chief Opposers of the same Church and Faith. Written by a Prisoner of the Baptized Churches in Lincolnshire. [s. l.] 8°. [*Taylor*, i: 198; *Watt*, s. n.]   263

1662. Propositions concerning the Subject of Baptism, and Consociation of Churches, etc. by a Synod at Boston in New England, etc. Cambridge, N. E. 4°, pp. 48.
B. M. [701. i. 9. (1.)]   264

1662. C. CHAUNCY. — *Anti-Synodalia Scripta Americana*; or a Proposal of the Judgment of the Dis- senting Messengers of the Churches of N. England, etc. Cambridge, N. E. 4°, pp. 38.
[Mass. Hist. Soc. Lib.]   265

1663. J. DAVENPORT. — Another Essay for Investigation of the Truth in Ansvver to Two Questions, concerning (1) The Svbject of Baptism, (2) the Consociation of Churches, etc. Cambridge, N. E. 4°, pp. xvi, 72.
B. M. [4183. aa.] 266

1663. T. SHEPARD. — The Church-membership of Children, and their Right to Baptisme. Cambridge, N. E. 4°, pp. xxii, 26.
Prince Library, [27. 83.] 267

1664. [B. KEACH.] — The Child's Instructor: or, a new and easy Primmer, etc. 16°. [teaches that infants should not be baptized, etc.] [*Crosby*, ii: 186.] 268

1664. J. ALLIN. — Animadversions upon the *Antisynodalia* [no. 265], etc. in the name of the Dissenting Brethren, etc. Cambridge, N. E. 4°, pp. vi, 82.
Prince Library, [27. 85.] 269

1664. [J. MITCHELL & R. MATHER.] — A Defence of the Answer and Arguments of the Synod met at Boston in the year 1662, concerning the Svbject of Baptism, etc. . . . against the Keplv made thereto by the Rev. Mr. J. Davenport . . . in his Treatise entituled *Another Essay* [no. 266], etc. Cambridge, N. E. 4°, pp. ii, 46, 102.
B. M. [701. i. 9. (2.)] 270

1665. J. IVES. — Infant Baptism Disproved, and Believers Baptism Proved, etc. 4°. [*Watt*, s. n.] 271

1665. Collection of the Testimonies of the Fathers of the New England Churches respecting Baptism, etc. Cambridge, N. E. 4°, pp. 32. [*Trans. Amer. Antiq. Soc.* vi: 315.] 272

1668. [J. S.][COTTOW.] — Translation of a portion of G. de Brez's Rise, Spring and Foundation of the Anabaptists, or Rebaptized of our Times, etc. Cambridge, N. E. 4°, pp. 52.
[Dr. Williams's Library.] 273

1669. T. WALL. — A Necessary Treatise for this age, or a Plain Discovery of that great Error of Denying Baptisme with Water to the Children of Believers, etc. 16°, pp. 52.
B. M. [1018. c. 13. (1.)] 274

1669. M. CRAFORDIUS. — Exercitatio Apologetica. Pro doctrina de perpetua obligatione quarti præcepti de Sabbato, ab Ecclesiis Reformatis communiter recepta, etc. adversus Socinianos, Anabaptistas, etc. Ultraject. 8°.
[I have it.] 275

[1670.] J. NORCOTT. — Baptism Discovered Plainly and Faithfully According to the Word of God, etc. 4°. [several times reprinted, *e.g.* 1694, 1721, 1722, 1723, 1878.] 276

1670. J. WHISTON. — Infant Baptism from Heaven, and not of Men, etc. 8°, pp. xlvi, 320.
B. M. [4323. a. (1.)] 277

1671. T. LAWSON. — A Treatise concerning Baptism; with a Discourse concerning the Supper-Bread and wine called also Communion, etc. 4°. [*Watt*, s. n.] 278

1672. [T. R.][UDVARD.] — The Anabaptists Lying Wonder attested by his Brother Independent, returned upon themselves, etc. 4°, pp. 16.
B. M. [4151. b.] 279

1672. [T. R.][UDVARD.] — The Anabaptist Preacher unmask'd, in a further Discovery of his Lying Wonder out of Lincolnshire : as also the News from Richard Hobbs, an Anabaptist Preacher in Dover, examined. Their juggles, Lyes, and Deceits detected, etc. 4°, pp. 20.
B. M. [110. j. 242. (3.)] 280

1672. L. HOWARD. — A Looking Glass for the Baptists, etc. [*Taylor*, i : 99, etc.] 281

1672. G. WHITEHEAD. — The Dipper Plunged: or, Thomas Hicks his feigned *Dialogue between a Christian and a Quaker*, etc. proved an unchristian forgery, etc. 4°, pp. 20. [Smith's *Friends Books*, ii : 893.] 282

1672. [E. N.] — Truth is strongest, or Infant Baptism once more soberly Examined, fairly Tryed and justly Censured. Being Reflections on two sermons by Mr. Sharp on behalf of J. B. etc. 4°. 283

1673. H. COLLINS. — An Antidote to prevent the Prevalency of Anabaptism, etc. 4°. [*Watt*, s. n.] 284

1673. Mr. Baxter Baptized in Bloud, or, a Sad History of the Unparallel'd Cruelty of the Anabaptists in New England. Faithfully Relating the Cruel, Barbarous, and Bloudy Murther of Mr. Baxter an Orthodox Minister, who was kill'd by the Anabaptists, and his skin most cruelly flead off from his Body, etc. 4°, pp. 6.
[One sold in the Brinley Collection.] 285

1673. Forgery Detected, and Innocency Vindicated: Being a faithfull account of the seasonable Discovery of an horrid and detestible slander raised on the Anabaptists of New England, in that diabolical pamphlet entituled *Mr. Baxter* [no. 285], etc. 4°, pp. 16.
B. M. [4323. b.] 286

1673. J. BUNYAN. — Differences in Judgment about Water Baptism no bar to Communion, etc. 8°, pp. 122. [" Here is also Mr. H. Jesses Judgment," etc.]
B. M. [4327. b.] 287

1674. T. PLANT. — An Account of the two Meetings at Barbican and Wheeler's Street, on account of the Quakers' Appeal to the Baptists against Thomas Hicks [see no. 282], etc. 4°. [*Ivimey*, ii: 443.] — 288

1674. B. KEACH. — Mr. Baxter's Arguments for Believers Baptism, etc. [single sheet.] [*Crosby*, iv: 276.] — 289

1674. T. GRANTHAM. — The Loyal Baptist; or an Apology for the Baptized Believers, etc. [*Watt*, s. n. *Crosby*, iv: vi.] — 290

1674. D. DYKE. — The Quakers Appeal Answered; or, a full Relation of the occasion, progress, and issue of a meeting at Barbican between the Baptists and the Quakers, etc. 8°. [*Crosby*, i: 359.] — 291

1674. H. D'ANVERS. — A Treatise of Baptism, etc. 8°, pp. xlviii, 388. B. M. [874. d. 34. (1.)] — 292

1674. J. GRATTAN. — John Baptist Decreasing, and Christ increasing, etc. 8°. [cited by Barclay, *Inner Life*, etc. p. 378.] — 293

1674. O. WILLS. — Infant Baptism asserted and vindicated by Scripture, and Antiquity: in answer to H. D. [no 292], etc. Bodleian, [8°, Z. 22. Th.] — 294

1675. I. MATHER. — The First Principles of New England, concerning the Subject of Baptisme & Communion of Churches, etc. Cambridge, N. E. 4°, pp. viii, 40, 8. B. M. (4183. b.] — 295

1675. I. MATHER. — A Discourse concerning the Subject of Baptisme, Wherein the present Controversies, etc. in the New England Churches are enquired into. Cambridge, N. E. 4°, pp. iv, 76. Bodleian, [Mather, 4°, 10.] — 296

1675. Fifty Queries seriously propounded to those who question or deny Infants right to Baptism. 12°. [Dr. Williams's Library.] — 297

1675. O. WILLS. — *Vindiciæ Vindiciarum*: or, a Vindication of a late Treatise, entituled, *Infant Baptism Asserted* [no. 294], etc. 16°, pp. viii, 200. Bodleian, [8°, Z. 22. Th.] — 298

1675. R. BAXTER. — More Proofs of Infant Church-Membership, and consequently of their right to Baptism, etc. 8°, pp. xiv, 414. B. M. [4326. b.] — 299

1675. Arguments Pro and Con about the right of Baptizing: Whether it ought to be by putting the whole Body under water, etc. [single sheet.] fol. B. M. [816. m. 24. (24.)] — 300

1675. R. BLINMAN. — A Rejoynder to Mr. Henry D'Anvers his Brief Friendly Reply to my Answer about Infant Baptism, etc. 24°. [*Allibone*, s. n.] — 301

1675. T. GRANTHAM. — Mr. Horne Answered; or, Pædo-Rantism not from Zion; wherein is shewed his mistake about the reason of his writing; and the insufficiency of his evidence alledged to prove Infant-Baptism descended from Zion [no. 183], briefly discovered, etc. 4°, pp. 30. [*Taylor*, i: 432.] — 302

1675. D. DYKE. — The Baptists Answer to Mr. Wills' Appeal (no. 294], etc. 8°. [*Crosby*, i: 359.] — 303

1675. J. TOMBES. — A Just Reply to the books of Mr. Wills (no. 294] and Mr. Blinman (no. 301], for Infant-baptism; in a Letter to Henry D'Anvers, Esq. 8°. [*Crosby*, i: 297.] — 304

1676. J. WHISTON. — An Essay to revive the Primitive Doctrine and Practice of Infant Baptism. 8°. Bodleian, [8°, Z. 23. Th.] — 305

1676. R. BAXTER. — A Review of the State of Christian Infants, etc. 12°. Bodleian, [8°, C. 125. Th.] — 306

1676. E. HUTCHINSON. — A Treatise concerning the Covenant and Baptism Dialogue-wise, between a Baptist and a Pædo-baptist; wherein is shewed that Believers only are the Spirituall seed of Abraham . . . with some animadversions upon a book Intituled *Infant Baptism from Heaven* [no. 277], etc. 8°, pp. xxviii, 108. B. M. [874. d. 32.] — 307

1676. 'W RUSSELL. — An Epistle concerning Baptism, in answer to two Treatises published by Mr. T. James, Teacher of a Congregation at Ashford in Kent, etc. [*Crosby*, iv: 261.] — 308

1676. W. ALLEN. — A Friendly Address to the Nonconformists, beginning with the Anabaptists, etc. 8°. [*Watt*, s. n.] — 309

1676. O. WILLS. — A Censure of the Sentence of the Baptists upon an Appeal made against H. D'Anvers. 4°. [*Watt*, s. n.] — 310

1676. T. DELAUNE. — Mr. R. Baxter's *Review of the State of Christian Infants* [no. 306], etc. examined, etc. 12°. [Dr. Williams's Library.] — 311

1677.	W. WALKER. — A Modest Plea for Infants Baptism, Wherein the lawfulness of the baptizing of Infants is defended against the Anti-pædobaptists, etc. Cambridge, 8°. B. M. [4323. aa.]	312
1677.	A Confession of Faith, Put forth by the Elders and Brethren of many Congregations of Christians (baptized upon Profession of their Faith) in London, and the country, etc. 16°, pp. xiv, 142. B. M. [3505. aa. 6.]	313
1678.	[J. ST. NICHOLAS.] — The History of Baptism, or, One Faith, one Baptism, in the several Editions thereof, under Noah, Moses, Christ; with an Appendix, entitled *Baptismus Redivivus*, etc. 8°, pp. viii, 29, vi, 108, xxix. Prince Library, [12. 40. 41.]	314
1678.	An Abstract of Mr. Baxter's *Plain Scripture Proof* [nos. 135, 299], etc. 12°. [Dr. Williams's Library.]	315
1678.	Some Brief Directions for Improvement of Infant Baptism, etc. 12°. [Dr. Williams's Library.]	316
1678.	T. GRANTHAM. — *Christianismus Primitivus*; or the Ancient Christian Religion, etc. [*Watt*, s. n.]	317
1678.	W. WALKER. — The Doctrine of Baptisms, or a Discourse of Dipping and Sprinkling, etc. 8°. [*Watt*, s. n.]	318
1679.	J. ELIOT. — A Brief Answer to a Small Book written by John Norcot [no. 276] against Infant-Baptisme. This Answer is written by John Eliot for the Sake of Some of the Flock of Jesus Christ who are ready to be staggered in point of *Infant Baptism* by reading his Book. Boston, N. E. 8°, pp. ii, 28. [A copy was sold with the Brinley Collection, which fetched $130.00.]	319
1680.	S. MATHER. — An *Irenicum*; or an essay for union between Presbyterians, Independents and Anabaptists, etc. 4°. Bodleian, [Ashm. 1210. (4.)]	320
1680.	T. GRANTHAM. — Epistle for Plain Truth and Peace between the Protestants of the Church of England and those of the Baptized Believers, etc. 8°. [*Watt*, s. n.]	321
1680.	R. RICH — The Epistles of Mr. Robert Rich to the seven Churches (so called by him), viz.: (1) To the Roman Catholics; (2) The Episcopal Protestant; (3) The Presbyterian; (4) The Independent; (5) The Anabaptist; (6) The Quaker; (7) The Church of the First Born, etc. 4°, pp. xx, 116. B. M. [4151. aaaa. (6.)]	322
1680.	I. MATHER. — The Divine Right of Infant-Baptisme Asserted and Proved from Scripture and Antiquity, etc. 4°, pp. viii, 28. B. M. [4323. aaa.]	323
1680.	T. GRANTHAM. — The Controversie about Infants Church Membership and Baptism epitomized, etc. 4°, pp. 36. B. M. [4325. aaa.]	324
1681.	S. WILLARD. — *Ne Sutor ultra Crepidam*. Or Brief Animadversions upon the New-England Anabaptists late Fallacious Narrative [see Backus's *Hist. N. Eng.* i: 490]; wherein the Notorious Mistakes and Falsehoods by them Published, are detected. Boston, N. E. 4°, pp. viii, 28. B. M. [4183. b.]	325
1681.	The Leacherous Anabaptist: or, The Dipper Dipt. A New Protestant Ballad, etc. [single sheet] fol. B. M. [1872. a. 1. (91.)]	326
1681.	N. COXE. — A Discourse of the Covenants that God made with Men before the Law; wherein the Covenant of Circumcision is more largely handled, and the Invalidity of the Plea for Pædobaptism taken from thence discovered, etc. 8°. [*Ivimey*, ii: 405.]	327
1681.	W. KIFFIN. — A Sober Discourse of Right to Church Communion, wherein is proved . . . that no unbaptized Person may be regularly admitted to the Lord's Supper, etc. 4°. [*Ivimey*, iii: 315.]	328
1681.	N. COLLINS. — A Sermon Preached at the Ordination of an Elder and Deacon in a Baptist Congregation in London, etc. 4°, pp. 40. [Mass. Histor. Soc.'s Library.]	329
1683.	N. TAYLOR. — The Baptism of Infants Vindicated, etc. 8°. [Dr. Williams's Library.]	330
1683.	[G. FIRMIN.] — The Plea of Children of Believing Parents for their Interest in Abraham's Covenant, their Right to Church-membership with their parents, etc. in answer to Mr. D'Anvers [no. 292], etc. [Dr. Williams's Library.]	331
1683.	G. HICKES. — The Case of Infant Baptism, in Five Questions, etc. 4°, pp. ii, 94. [*Quest.* 3: "Whether is it lawful to separate from a Church which appointeth Infants to be Baptized?"] B. M. [701. i. 9. (3.)]	332

1684. R. BURTHOGGE. — Arguments for Infant Baptism, etc. 8°. 333
[Dr. Williams's Library]

[1685.] [T. GRANTHAM.] — The Baptists Complaint against the Persecuting Priests, etc. [MS.] [*Crosby*, 334
iii: 54; *Taylor*, i: 208.]

1687. G. TOWERSON. — Of the Sacrament of Baptism in particular; of the right of Baptism among the 335
Heathens and Jews, and of the Institution of Christian Baptism, etc. [*Watt*, s. n.]

1687. T. GRANTHAM. — Presumption no Proof, etc. 4°. [a reply against Infant-baptism to Mr. Petto and 336
Mr. Firmin.] [*Taylor*, i: 213.]

1687. T. GRANTHAM. — Hear the Church: or, an Appeal to the Mother of us all. Being an Epistle to 337
all the Baptized Believers in England, etc. 4°. [*Taylor*, i: 214.]

1687. Infant Baptism of Christ's Appointment, etc. 12°. 338
[Dr. Williams's Library.]

1687. O. HEYWOOD. — Baptismal Bonds Renewed; being some Meditations on Ps. l: 5, etc. 12°. 339
B. M. [3090. b.]

1688. W. PARDOE — Ancient Christianity Revived; being a Description of the Doctrine, Discipline, and 340
Practice of the little City Bethania, etc. . . . By one of her Inhabitants, who desireth to worship
God after the way which some men call heresie, etc. 12°. [*Ivimey*, ii: 580.]

[1688.] Three Considerations proposed to Mr. W. Penn, concerning the Validity and Security of his new 341
Magna Charta for Liberty of Conscience. By a Baptist. 4°.
B. M. [T. 692. (6.)]

1688. An Answer by an Anabaptist to the *Three Considerations* [no. 341], etc. by a pretended Baptist, 342
etc. 8°.
Bodleian, [G. Pamph. 1785. (4.)]

1688. G. FIRMIN. — Scripture-Warrant Sufficient Proof for Infant-Baptism, etc. 4°. 343
[Dr. Williams's Library.]

1688. T. GRANTHAM. — The Infants Advocate, etc. in answer to a book of Mr. G. F.'s, entitled *Scripture* 344
Warrant [no. 343], etc. 4°.
B. M. [4323. b.]

1689. P. TILLINGHAST. — Water-Baptism Plainly Proved by Scripture to be a Gospel Precept, etc. 4°, 345
pp. 16.
[Amer. Antiqn. Soc.'s Library.]

1689. B. KEACH. — Gold Refin'd; or Baptism in its Primitive Purity . . . in which it is clearly evinced 346
that Baptism is not Aspersion, etc. 16°, pp. viii, 184.
B. M. [4326. a.]

1689. A Narrative of the Proceedings of the General Assembly of Divers Pastors, Messengers, and Min- 347
istring Brethren of the Baptized Churches, met together in London from Sept. 3 to 12, 1689, etc.
owning the Doctrine of Personal Election and final Perseverance. Sent from and concerned for
more than one hundred congregations, etc. 4°, pp. 30.
B. M. [4139. c.]

1689. T. GRANTHAM. — A Friendly Debate concerning Infant Baptism, being an answer to Dr. Hickes 348
Case [no. 332], etc. 4°.
[Dr. Williams's Library.]

1689. G. FIRMIN. — An Answer to the vain and unprofitable Question put to him, and charged upon him 349
by Mr. Grantham in his book intituled *The Infants Advocate* [no. 344], etc. 4°.

1689. T. GRANTHAM. — Truth and Peace; or the last and most Friendly Debate concerning Infant Bap- 350
tism, etc. 8°. [*Taylor*, i: 316.]

[1689.] J. OWEN. — Infant Baptism from Heaven, etc. [in Welsh.] [*Ivimey*, ii: 385.] 351

[1689.] B. KEACH. — Light broke forth in Wales, etc. in reply to Mr. Owen's *Infant* [no. 351], etc. [in 352
Welsh and English.] [*Ivimey*, ii: 385.]

1690. [MR. CARY.] — A Solemne Call to Baptisme, etc. 8°. [*Watt*, s. n.] 353

1690. T. WALL. — Baptism Anatomized: being Propounded in five Queries, viz.: (1) What Water Bap- 354
tism is? (2) What is the end for which it is instituted? (3) What giveth right to it? (4) Who are the
true administrators of it? (5) Whether it be lawful for a man to baptize himself? 8°.

1690. J. WHISTON. — The right method for the Proving of Infant-Baptism. With reflections on some 355
late Tracts on Infant Baptism, etc. 8°, pp. 72.
Bodleian, [Pamph. 198.]

1690. A Brief History of the Rise, Growth, Reign, Supports and Sodain fatal Foyl of Popery, during the 356
years and an half of James the Second, etc. Together with a Description of the Six Popish Pillars:
the Anabaptists, Presbyterians, Quakers, Independents, Roman-Catholicks & Popish Churchmen,
etc. 4°, pp. ii, 34.
Bodleian, [Pamph. 199.]

1690. Primitive Baptism, and therein Infants and Parents right. 12°. 357
Bodleian, [8°, Z. 267. Th.]

1691. H. COLLINS. — Believers-Baptism from Heaven, and of Divine institution; Infants-Baptism from 358
earth and human invention. Proved from the Commission of Christ, etc. with a Brief, yet sufficient Answer to T. Wall's book called *Baptism Anatomized* [no. 354], etc. 16°, pp. ii, 140.
B. M. [4323. a.]

1691. S. PETTO. — Infant-Baptism Vindicated from the exceptions of Thomas Grantham [no. 336?], 359
etc. 8°.
B. M. [1018. d. 20. (2.)]

[1691.] J. FLAVEL. — A Treatise on Baptism, etc. 4°. 360

1691. A Narrative of the General Assembly of the Elders and Messengers of the Baptized Churches, sent 361
from divers parts of England and Wales, which began in London June 2, and ended on the 8th of
the same month, 1691, Owning the Doctrines of Personal Election and Final Perseverance, etc.
4°. [*Ivimey*, i: 311.]

1691. B. KEACH. — Pædo-Baptism. Being an answer to the Athenian Society, etc. 4°. [*Crosby*, vi: 312.] 362

1691. T. GRANTHAM. — A Dialogue between the Baptist and the Presbyterian, etc. 4°, pp. 50. [*Taylor*, i: 482.] 363

1692. T. WALL. — Infants-Baptism from Heaven, of divine institution: being a brief yet satisfactory 364
Answer to some objections made by H. Collins in his book entituled *Believer's Baptism* [no. 358],
etc. 16°, pp. 40.
B. M. [4326. bb.]

[1692.] W. BURKIT. — An Argumentative and Practical Discourse of Infant Baptism, etc. [*Ivimey*, 365
ii: 367.]

1692. B. KEACH. — The Rector rectified, or, Infants Baptism unlawful. Being an Answer to Mr. Burkit 366
[no. 365], etc. 8°. [*Crosby*, vi: 312.]

[1692.] E. ROTHWELL. — A Vindication of Presbyterian Ordination and Baptism, etc. 8°. 367

1692. M. STRONG. — The Indecency and Unlawfulness of Baptizing Children in Private, etc. 4°. [*Watt*, 368
s. n.]

[1692.] G. SHUTE. — An Antidote to prevent the Prevalency of Anabaptism, etc. 4°. 369

1693. A Copy of a Brief Treatise of the proper subjects and Administration of Baptism, etc. 12°. 370
[Dr. Williams's Library.]

1693. P. STUBS. — A Sermon on Publick Baptism before the Lord Mayor of London, etc. 4°. 371
Bodleian, [C. 5 12. Linc.]

1693. A Narrative of the Proceedings of the Elders, Messengers and Ministering Brethren of divers bap- 372
tized Churches in England and Wales, holding the doctrines of Particular Election and Final Perseverance, in their General Assembly at Bristol on the 19th of the second month, called April,
1693, and continued to the 21st. of the same. Also, containing the Proceedings of the General
Assembly held in London the 6th day of the 4th month, called June, and continued till the 12th of
the same, etc. 4°. [*Ivimey*, i: 524.]

1693. J. EXELL. — A Serious Inquiry into Infant Baptism, shewing, by plain Scripture Proof, that John 373
Baptist did as certainly baptize Infants as Adults, etc. 4°. [*Watt*, s. n.]

1693. H. COLLINS. — The *Antidote* [no. 369] proved a Counterfeit, or Error Detected, and Believers Baptism Vindicated, etc. 4°. [*Watt*, s. n.] 374

1693. B. KEACH. — The Ax laid to the Root; or one Blow more at the Foundation of Infant's Baptism 375
and Church Membership. 4°. [*Crosby*, vi: 312.]

1693. B. KEACH. — The Ax laid to the Root, Part II. wherein Mr. Flavel's [no. 360]; Mr. Rothwell's 376
[no. 367], and Mr. Exell's [no. 373] Arguments are answered, etc. 4°. [*Crosby*, vi: 312.]

1693. The Lynn Persecution, etc. 4°. [*Taylor*, i: 215.] 377

1693. C. DOE. — The Reason why not Infant-Sprinkling, but Believers Baptism ought to be approved, etc. 378
. . . To which is added How Infant Sprinkling came in Fashion: The Evil Tendencies of Infant
Sprinkling: Differences between Believers Baptism and Infant Sprinkling, etc. 16°, pp. 84.
[Mass. Hist. Soc.'s Lib.]

1694. J. OLLYFFE, — A Brief Defence of Infant Baptism, with an Appendix, etc. 4°. 379
B. M [478. a. 29. (3.)]

[1694] G. FIRMIN — Some Remarks upon the Anabaptists Answer to the Athenian Mercuries, etc. 4°. 380
[*N. E. Hist. & Gen. Reg.* xxv: 56.]

1694. B. KEACH. — A Counter Antidote: or, an Answer to Shute's *Antidote to prevent the Prevalency of* 381
Anabaptism [no. 369], etc. 4°. [*Crosby*, vi: 312.]

1695.	G. SHUTE. — Infant Baptism and Church Membership proved; and also the Mode of Baptism to be by Sprinkling, etc. 12°. Bodleian, [Pamph. 218.]	382
1695.	W. ASSHETON. — Conference with an Anabaptist, etc. 18°.	383
[1695.]	H. COLLINS. — The Sandy Foundation of Infants Baptism shaken, etc. 4°. [*Crosby*, iii: 130.]	384
1696.	M. HARRISON. — Infant Baptism God's Ordinance, etc. With a Rebuke of several erroneous opinions the Arminian Anabaptists hold concerning Original Sin, etc. being an answer to the Anabaptists, and Mr. Collins his *Sandy Foundation* [no. 384], etc. 16°, pp. xiv, 50. Prince Library, [28. 32.]	385
1696.	R. BARCLAY. — Baptism and the Lord's Supper substantially asserted. Being an Apology in behalf of the People called Quakers concerning these two heads, etc. 8°, pp. 68. [Amer. Antiqn. Soc. Library.]	386
1697.	E. KEACH. — A Short Confession of Faith, containing the substance of the Larger, put forth by the Elders of the Baptized Churches, etc. 24°. [Brown University Library.]	387
1698.	G. KEITH. — The Arguments of the Quakers, more particularly, of G. Whitehead, W. Penn, R. Barclay, etc. against Baptism and the Supper, examined and refuted, etc. 4°, pp. 120. B. M. [4152. e.]	388
1698.	A Discourse on Infant Baptism, by way of Dialogue, etc. 12°. [Dr. Williams's Library.]	389
[1698–9.]	[W. RUSSELL.] — A True Narrative of the Portsmouth Disputation between some Ministers of the Presbyterians, and others of the Baptist persuasion, concerning the Subjects and Manner of Baptism, etc. 4°. [*Crosby*, iii: 313.]	390
1699.	S. CHANDLER, W. LEIGH & B. ROBINSON. — An Impartial Account of the Portsmouth Disputation. With some just Reflections on Dr. Russell's Pretended Narrative [no. 390], etc. with an healing Preface to the sober Anabaptists. 8°, pp. xvi, 102. [I have it.]	391
1699.	A Confession of Faith put forth by the Elders and Brethren of many Congregations of Christians, (baptized upon profession of their faith) in London and the Country, etc. 24°, pp. xxiv, 106, ii. [another edition of no. 313.]	392
1699.	[F. CATROU.] — Histoire des Anabaptistes; contenant leur Doctrine, les diverses Opinions, qui les divisant en plusieurs sects, les Troubles, qu'ils ont causez, et enfin tout ce qui s'est passé de plus considerable à leur egard, depuis l'an 1521 jusques à present. Amsterdam, 12°. B. M. [856. f. 15.]	393
1699.	J. TURNER. — A Vindication of Infant Baptism, etc. 4°. [*Watt*, s. n.]	394
1699.	T. HEWERDINE. — Some Plain Letters in the Defense of Infant Baptism, etc. 8°. [*Watt*, s. n.]	395
1700.	W. RUSSELL. — Infant Baptism is Will-Worship; being a Confutation of the Answer to the Portsmouth Disputation [no. 391], etc. 4°. [*Crosby*, iv: 261.]	396
1700.	R. HOLLAND. — A Sermon at the Baptizing of some Persons of Riper Years, on Acts ii: 38, etc. 4°. [*Watt*, s. n.]	397
1700.	[T. OATES.] — New Discovery: being his Letters to the Church of the Baptists, etc. 4°. [*Watt*, s. n.]	398
[1700.]	Agreement of the Associated Ministers of the County of Essex [Eng.] as to Baptism, etc. 4°. [Bowdoin College Library.]	399
1700.	E. HITCHIN. — The Infants Cause Vindicated, etc. 8°. [Dr. Williams's Library.]	400
[1700.]	D. RUSSEN. — Fundamentals without a Foundation; or a true picture of the Anabaptists.	401

www.ingramcontent.com/pod-product-compliance
Lightning Source LLC
Chambersburg PA
CBHW030405170426
43202CB00010B/1498